MEET ME THERE

I0659091

GAIL ASHTON
JOHN BARNIE
MARK CHARLTON
JAN FORTUNE
IAN GREGSON
MAVIS GULLIVER
HAZEL MANUEL
JANE McKIE
JIM PERRIN
SUSAN RICHARDSON

GAIL ASHTON (editor)

CinnamonPress
INDEPENDENT INNOVATIVE INTERNATIONAL

Published by Cinnamon Press,
Meirion House,
Tanygrisiau,
Blaenau Ffestiniog,
Gwynedd
LL41 3SU
www.cinnamonpress.com

ISBN 978-1-909077-81-2
British Library Cataloguing in Publication Data. A CIP record for this book can be obtained from the British Library.

Designed and typeset in Garamond by Cinnamon Press.
Cover design by Adam Craig © Adam Craig

Cinnamon Press is represented by Inpress
and by the Welsh Books Council in Wales.

The publisher gratefully acknowledges the support of the Welsh Books Council.

Printed in Poland

Acknowledgements

So many thanks to all the people who made this book happen either by writing a chapter, contributing to the Introduction, or just by talking to me or offering something to read. If I miss your name here, my apologies: John Barnie, Mark Charlton, Jenny Cooke, Mim Darlington, Jan Fortune, Sue Gregory, Ian Gregson, Mavis Gulliver, Emily Hinshelwood, Chris Kinsey, Karen Maitland, Hazel Manuel, John McAuliffe, Jane McKie, Louisa Adjoa Parker, Jim Perrin, Sue Richardson, Frances Sackett, Joy Winkler.

Special thanks too to Jan Fortune and the Cinnamon Press team who, as ever, made this a joy to work on: congratulations on taking Cinnamon Press so far without ever losing its sense of place or family. To Jan in particular, warmest gratitude and heartfelt thanks simply for being what every Cinnamon author knows — the most amazing editor, the one who always takes you safely home.

Contents

This book is dedicated, with so much love,
to my sister Nettie who holds me in place
even when it seems nothing else can

Meet Me There.

Introduction: Meet Me There
Gail Ashton

It is not enough to inhabit a place. Thanks to the fast-paced transitory nature of contemporary lives and cultures, most of us no longer 'know a place deeply.' Instead we are 'disconnected from the physical places in which we live,' abandon them with ease — for new jobs, a lover, new distractions. Naomi Klein is here talking of how we so often miss the incremental and insidious signs of climate change, most of it local and specific, the late arrival of a migratory bird, say, or early flowering of a particular bloom. But I am struck by the parallels with our 21st century dismissal of the importance of place. Place is fundamental to our physical and psychological well-being. It offers more than shelter. Who can forget those almost daily news images of refugees fleeing famine and war, or of survivors of natural and human-made disaster, their faces, that shock register of displacement from land, home, culture, family? Perhaps, like me, you recall first hand soul-destroying urban estates with their rat-runs and no-goes, or rioting cities burning into the night. Maybe your homelands have been invaded by second-comers, your places misunderstood or usurped, your place in the world called into question. You may have moved on, or been moved on. Either way you might have forgotten what Wendell Berry tells Klein: 'Stop somewhere...And begin the 1,000 year-long process of knowing that place.'

Some people still do that. In 2004 a tsunami hit the Asian seaboard. Over 230,000 people were killed in coastal communities across fourteen countries by waves reaching up to 100 feet. The Moken were not amongst them. One of Thailand's tribes of nomadic sea-gypsies, the Moken's oral stories had been predicting the arrival of the *laboon* for generations. Such tales are shaped by a cultural and linguistic landscape through which the Moken recognise their place in the world. These people live in and out of the ocean, can swim before they can walk. They tell of a sea glass-smooth on that Boxing Day morning. Of hermit crabs scuttling out of water onto the shore and into the forest where not a single bird called or sang. Deep-sea fish began to rise to the surface. Divers told of dolphins moving en masse away from the coast. The Moken too knew to head for the depths or the mountains. They ran to the hills and survived.

We all know such things. It's just that mostly we have forgotten how to know. Unless you are a writer, of course. Emily Hinshelwood describes how:

> Place changes me. It affects my mood, my thoughts, my writing. Compare the still heavy air of an empty pub to a blustery hillside overlooking a choppy sea. Add an old flooded slate quarry where kids scream in somersaults off the crumbling engine house — and something deep inside me is triggered. I am drawn to this interaction of humans and nature; how we have changed the landscape, and how that landscape and those changes go on to transform us further.
>
> I like to imagine a place's disorganised, jerky past. I reflect on its present, full of sudden surprises and juxtapositions. Each place is an embodiment of everything that has happened there, up until this moment in time. And also everything that will happen there in the future.
>
> My being in this place becomes part of its history as well as part of my own history. Somehow that knowledge assists me as I inch through my life.

I walk through the landscape. I notice my movement in a changing world. I try to capture momentarily a glimpse of where and how I fit into this vast breadth of history. This is where my poetry begins.

Like the Moken Alan Garner knows his place. He defines himself as 'a man of his square mile/ dyn ei filltir sgwâr', in this case the Edge in Alderley Edge, Cheshire, not far from where I currently live and where his family have lived and worked for generations. Such rootedness, he says, is 'more than metaphor. It is symbiosis.' Garner's intimacy with this landscape is both actual and a fiction. As a teenager he ran far and wide. His body came to know 'the rhythms of the fields.' As a child he was often unwell. Confined to his room, his imagination played out alternate imaginative homescapes. Garner says, 'all I have written derives from the land on which I ran...And in the physical particulars and the spirit of that place I find the story.'

There are so many places from which to write, fictive or otherwise. To begin we need a space to call our own if our writerly imaginations are to flourish. Jenny Cooke tells it like this:

It's the same every year. Petals swirl round the pear tree. They fall like confetti, mixing with the strident yellows of fallen tulips, stamens knocked sideways into the dirt. Sweet wrappers and a discarded plant pot protect these bulbs, though a beer bottle pokes its broken neck up from the soil. Children's angry shouts vie with aircraft engines that tear the sky in two. When her son kicks a punctured football at a tree stump, a row of toads are discovered, sheltering.

When can I write?

Once, a boy sauntered in from the next road. He spat. He never came again. Meanwhile her toddlers became juniors who climbed the tree above the shed and rode it like a horse. Her son morphed into a six-foot boy-man, still willing to toss a shuttlecock with his mother around the lawn. His father, of course, was always at the factory.

Will there ever be time?

Today, while seagulls scream and fight over broken bread chucked onto the grass, her son flings clothes into a suitcase.

She notices a self-seeded viola, muted in the border. It's dripping with flowers, unharmed by shards of glass.

Now?

For me Woolf's 'room of one's own' might be anywhere. No, I lie. What I need is head space, and time. I like the idea of *home*, am rattled by change and temporary transits. This need for peace, security, positive energy is part of the myriad ways in which we put down roots and connect with the places we inhabit. Mostly these connections are hugely personal. Jim Perrin confesses to 'sentimental yearnings at times' for his roots in Wales even as he's constantly drawn to 'the good place', his house 'in the foothills of the Pyrenees' where he 'can work easily and well.' We are all sensitive to atmosphere, though many have forgotten that primeval awareness. So, too, we have all felt *out of place* in some places, heard the prick of an untold story lurking somewhere at our back. Perhaps writers are unusually susceptible to this kind of awareness. As a young child my first 'writing' experiences came about as a result of a ghost in what was then our house in Devon Crescent. More recently, standing out of the way at a strangely deserted Rievaulx Abbey I turned from a corner of ruined stone and knew someone, or something, was at my back. I spoke out loud: *no you don't*. There is a story in there somewhere. Karen Maitland describes something similar:

> I believe that some places retain imprints of events or people. Just as photographic film retains a negative image when exposed to light, certain places become imprinted when exposed to intense emotion. Places that have been loved radiate an intense peace, others, where a tragedy has occurred, retain that pain and grief. Once, in a foreign city, I crossed a certain point in a street, which looked no different from the rest of the road. I was suddenly overwhelmed by misery and began to sob like a baby. When I retraced my footsteps the mood lifted instantly. Later I discovered the spot I had walked into had been the unmarked site of a terrible massacre of women and children in World War II.

Some places are far flung, wide contexts and habitats.

Or they might be small localised places, our own 'square mile' of constructed territory. Chris Kinsey says:

I like to be where glaciers were, on water meadows in altered river valleys and amongst sculpted hills. I can only reconcile myself to flat places for short visits and feel estranged in densely built environments. No matter how stunning the architecture is, I soon start pining for the wilds.

Though some contemporary writing — including chapters in this book — speaks much of the natural world this not the only impetus for a writer. Like many others, Mark Charlton, Ian Gregson and myself have much to say on working class, suburban places. Nor is the idea of place a simple context for a piece of work: think du Maurier's *Rebecca*. Karen Maitland says:

> I always regard the place where I set my novels as one of my main characters in the book, whether it's a town, a marshland or a room. As a character, the place has a personality and varying moods. It changes over time. The human characters interact with it and it shapes their personalities, their lives and the choices they make. For me, a place is not a passive backdrop to the action in my novels, but an active, living creature.

Sometimes that living creature goes by the name of *home*, even if it is not. Chris Kinsey writes:

> Growing up in Leominster, Herefordshire, my first friends were rivers. (The Welsh name for the town is Llanllienni, one translation of which is Land of Streams.) Before I started school, streams invited me out to play and set me exploring every day. I yearned to seek their sources in the Welsh hills. When I was nine, we travelled over Kerry Hill on our way to Barmouth. Just on the watershed between the source of the Teme and the Mule I saw a raven clinging to a fence post. Both pointed north over the Severn valley to the distant blue mountains of Aran Fawddwy and Cader Idris and I made a pact — *when I grow up I want to live near here* — and I have.

Joy Winkler tells of a similar need to belong:

> Some days it's the childhood places that I wrap around me like the old cardigan I can never bring

14

myself to throw away. These are places of handstands, rhymes and street games, of scythed wheat and the mysterious visiting fair. I can so easily bring to mind those fields, cracked pavements, old buildings and cinemas; memories stored in their soil, dust and echoes. Of course, there are always new places to be discovered; new friends in the wings, new beginnings. In the end though, it will always be the one I call *home* even though I moved away from it fifty years ago. This is truly the place where I belong.

How do we write of and through this sense that how we fit a place, and the place fits us, is a crucial and ancient drive? Sometimes we do it by defamiliarising a world or speaking of alienation or loss. Miriam Darlington's comment could have been epithet for almost any chapter in this book:

> How well do you know your patch, this land in all its wrinkles and dips and phases? How is your intimacy with it? Its water flows in our every cell and its soil is the iron in our blood. Where a place has been home, has caressed our senses in a familiar embrace, cradled us with its contours, accompanied us with all its voices, nurtured us in a mutual understanding, how do we deal with its loss?

That loss always turns out to be somewhere different from the place we imagined we knew. For writers especially, sometimes the places we inhabit aren't in the end as real as we would have them. Henry Moore's daughter recounts the moment she realised those pieces of art and sculpture her father had been producing with his failing eighty-odd year eyesight were not representations of their Hertfordshire home, as she'd thought, but 'memory landscapes' of his Yorkshire

15

roots. Helen Macdonald remarks similarly, how 'Even today some of my memories of landscapes turn out to be photographs' from the *AA Book of the Countryside* (1973) which had her family drive all over the UK on trips away from their home. It is through such sleights of eye, hand and mind that we seek to capture place. Mark Charlton tells me he went to check his 'facts' after writing his chapter for this volume. Then he realised these strange amalgams of recollection, reality and fictionalising sidestep and collude to make a more 'honest' truth than truth itself. Some days after this conversation about authenticity my father let slip that in my early childhood our house was but a hundred yards from Cannock Chase. We played on it, literally, daily, even though in my mind it had been much further than that.

In the end, perhaps all that matters is a certain quality of attention, something every writer and every chapter in this book shares. In one of our emails Jim Perrin talks of 'What lives unseen all around us!' It is this that writers sense for without it we cannot hear Alan Garner's 'the voice of the land.' That voice speaks to us in so many different ways, its language both known forever and acutely strange. Language and landscape are symbiotic; the one shapes the other, or, as Robert Macfarlane puts it, 'Words are grained into our landscapes, and landscapes grained into our words.' Some places are beyond articulation, their 'origins' obscured or simply lost. Others have names replete with hidden narratives and birth-stories. A name may appropriate but it also helps us to make sense of our place within a world. That same name may be singular and incomplete, precise and poetic, a disarticulation as much as a naming (think 'Not-Doctor Street' in Toni Morrison's *Song of Solomon*). For a place is always so much more than its name suggests, all those *Howards*

End, Brick Lane, Bleak House, NW, and *Wuthering Heights*, those historical, cultural and linguistic markers of place that are hidden narratives in themselves and which writers mine over and again. John McAuliffe expresses it thus:

My idea of any place's doubleness was formed in my home town, Listowel, a North Kerry market town like many other towns, which has long had a literary double life: the playwright John B Keane ran a pub on William Street and the fiction writer Bryan MacMahon, retired from school-teaching, could be seen walking the streets or sometimes leading a group of tourists around the town on Mart Day, describing its beauties, occasionally in French or Irish.

There was nothing extraordinary then about seeing John B in plain view as he took his daily walk by the River Feale: it was a mysterious and educational task, though, to square the writing with the fact of his wry, rheumy presence around town. He and Bryan McMahon wrote, unsentimentally, about the town's hinterland of farming villages and about the positive impact of modernity on old hierarchies: wised-up insiders with a natural sympathy for the outsider, they were a Kerry introduction to the doubleness of the writing life.

The connection between place and language was something I didn't really understand until after I'd moved away to England: now, driving along the Cork-Kerry border in Sliabh Luachra, I know I'm almost home when I see the signpost for O Rathaille's 'stick' (or school). O Rathaille, and Eoghan Rua O Suilleabhain, are emblematic figures for Kerry writers, eighteenth-century Irish-language poets whose writing lives were split apart by the shift in power and shift in language. One thing writers do is find the right names for places as well as for feelings and ideas, and sometimes the writing must just confess its own inadequacy to this task. Places exceed us, the old names tell us, or any new definitions we might wish upon these towns we leave and, every so often, return to.

How might we evoke place? What kinds of things do we pay attention to? What do we detail and how do we recreate that awareness, recall places that have personal resonance for us? Might we trust in memory with all its refractions, retractions, distractions? What of all those partisan and partial understandings of place, real, imagined or any combination of both? What of dissonance, the seductive charms of nostalgia? How does all of this make us the kinds of writers we become? These are the threads ten Cinnamon authors weave in this book. And what of imagination, to what extent are our fictions fictional? Frances Sackett says this:

> When I was a child I lived on the border of England and Wales; a place where the river Dee was lush with greenery and watercress grew in clumps. In the Spring primroses carpeted the banks like parings of the moon. The stone buildings in the village bred a silence that extended round the leafy backlanes and through the lych-gate of the church and cemetery. It has always retained a certain mystery for me; just as childhood seems a fantasy, this is a place for the imaginative spirit to inhabit.

Ultimately maybe this is all there is to take us onwards, to other places, to help us write up and into the stars:

I hear the low moan of the beasts. The light within the shippen is dim, the stalls in shadow but the churns and the tubing attached to the reddy-brown rubber teats glow softly. The light, the heady cow smell, moist straw and the warmth of the great black and white bodies make the scene swim before my eyes. I concentrate hard on the nearest cow's tail. It swells over the crusted rump and hangs loose, bedraggled as a dressing gown cord. 'It's going to be frosty,' Mr Worthington says. 'You'll walk home with the stars.'

We join the stony white track again. I slide my mittened hand into mum's great fur glove. Because it is dark I imagine it had snowed and that the fields folded round the lane sleep in flannelette sheets. They roll away into stone walls softened with bolsters and crystallised pine woods, into deep still pools under ice thick as marzipan, sugared over with snow. 'The stars *are* coloured at Christmas, aren't they?' I ask, very matter-of-fact.

'Where did you get that idea from, Susan?' Mum's hand squeezes mine for a moment.

[Sue Gregory, *Overton Farm*]

Eight years ago Oxford University Press faced public outrage over the compilation of its *Oxford Junior Dictionary*. Editors deleted entries considered irrelevant to contemporary children — *acorn, bluebell, catkin, conker, lark* — and replaced the natural world with a virtual one: *blog, broadband, chatroom, voicemail* (Macfarlane). Of course I deplore this loss, even as I realise that loss is an imperative for many writers. So, too, place is not a fixed entity or an essence but an idea and an ideal. It is at once boundless and bounded, elusive, allusive, even illusory. Its name is never the sum of its parts.

Such naming is part of a greater landscape than we might comprehend. Our awareness of place is filtered through landmarks and waymarks. We are flâneuses and pilgrim wayfarers both, and none more so than writers. We encounter images, artefacts, maps and constellations. We read books, guides, railway timetables. We are taught in school and out in the field, know ballads, songs, stories. Through all of these we mythologise and recount, pass on ancestral tales in dialects and out of them, in oral histories and in print. We pleat and twist, omit and amplify. Louisa Adjoa Parker writes of Lyme Regis, the darkness and the light:

> It is a place where land meets sea, a place of history, of fiction, where a grey stone wall curls around the harbour like an ammonite. Where dinosaurs come back to life, lift themselves up from the rock and roar. Where cliffs fall. Where boats are half-buried in wet sand when the tide is out, where the sea is bright and glittery as glass. Where curtains twitch, where gossip swells and falls like giant waves. Where white seagulls circle in the sky, mocking us with their cries. A place of narrow streets, of promenades, of pastel-coloured rows of beach huts, paint battered by sea spray. A place of rust and salt. In the summer a press of red-faced tourists on the white sand, sun umbrellas, wind breaks. Smells of sun-cream and fish and chips. In winter, there is nothing but the drifting ghosts of summers, rain, waves dropping pebbles on the promenade, bottles rattling in the wind. It is a place filled with memories, with tears that soaked into the sand and stones and bricks and grass. There are as many memories here as there are brown and grey pebbles on the beach. Perhaps more.

Lyme Regis might be anywhere. We commit to memory, revisit and re-imagine through a distorting but vivid lens. We hone and we forget, stay rooted and dissociate, bear witness and fail to pay attention. We pass on. We settle so that place is real, and not-real, familiar, and not-familiar. All these places, towns and villages, outlandish and known, new and blue-remembered, each one foreign to us every time we come again, each one necessary if we are to know our place, to learn how to keep us in place when we are so out of place for most of our lives. The chapters in this book tap into this web of ideas in unique ways to recreate places you might never have visited, to take us on voyages of their own.

Ever onwards. Come with me through the *eawl-leet*. Choose the journey, its mode of travel. Remember there are worlds within this book, and beyond. Let us reminisce, touch, listen to them. Watch for the fragmented, ever-morphing bleed at the edges of all the places we dream in and out of time. Track outshifts and aftermaths, the lost and the utopian, the cityscapes, earthscapes. Go north, south, east, west, skywards, sideways, underground. Scatter yourself to desert winds. Stand in the scald of a mountain storm. Catch yourself in the windhover of a moment. I ask only that you meet me there. I will be waiting.

Finding my Place
Mavis Gulliver

My mind's eye sees the garden of the house where I was born. Under the gnarled apple tree are clumps of snowdrops. The tree itself is bare — a tracery of branches scratching the sky, but the snowdrops are blooming. I tilt a flower to see the delicate green patterning of the inner petals. After the snowdrops there is a lull before deep pink buds burst into paler pink blossom. All too soon the petals drop, littering the grass as if snow has fallen. I watch as day on day the apples form and grow. I try to catch the windfalls, find it hard to wait for the fruit to ripen, for my teeth to break the skin, my tongue to taste the sharp sweetness. I see the swing, its green-painted seat with holes where the ropes pass through. I recall the joy of no longer needing a push to set me flying. Up into the air, thrilled at seeing beyond the garden, my horizons widening.

It is a place rooted in memory. Yet, years later I discover that we left the house when I was only three months old. So how had I formed and retained such a vivid sense of place? It was through words. My mum's description had made it live for me. When I discussed the memory with her I realised that her words were only partly responsible for the picture lodged so firmly in my head. She had given me words — apple tree, snowdrops and swing. In the years that followed the meaning of these words was enhanced through my own experience. I had grown snowdrops. I had watched the seasons come and go through other apple trees. I knew the swing because each time we moved house we took it with us. All this brought home to me the power of words, how a detailed description can transport the listener, or the reader, to a place that they have never seen.

Bombs fall on the Lincolnshire airfield where my dad is Clerk of Works. An air raid damages the hospital on the night I am born. Our hedge is set on fire by incendiary bombs. The next house is flattened. My dad has to stay, but for safety's sake we are sent to Clitheroe to live with my grandma. I only know these things by hearsay, but even now I cringe when a low-flying aircraft passes over. Is the sound rooted deeply in my memory? Was my mother's fear conveyed to me when I was a babe in arms? Whatever the reason, it is the strongest connection that I have with the place of my birth.

Shut Out The Sound

Over the hill they come, splitting the sky
with noise and hurtling speed.
Instinctively my fingers block my ears
pushing soft tissue tight against the drum.

My body, taut with fear, caught at my mother's breast
on the day she cowered beneath the table,
petrified that this first week of my life would be my
                                                    last.
Clutching me to her heart,
she could not free her hands to block her ears;
could not cut out the terrifying sound
of Spitfires and Messerschmidts
fighting overhead,
as a German bomber dropped his load
reducing the house next door
to rubble.
Nor could she still the thudding of her heart,
in the moment of stunned silence
that followed.

23

Where does my personal memory begin? It is in fleeting glimpses that are not recalled through hearsay or photographs; images that have imprinted themselves so strongly that they remain with me still. Such encounters are so intense that they can even have a direct influence on our future lives. I don't think it is a coincidence that my earliest memories are of flowers and sea, and that these have been at the core of my interests ever since.

Detailed memories elude me until I am four years old. We visit an aunt in Worcestershire. I am walking along a cinder path. The sharp-edged dusty fragments get into my sandals. I bend to empty them and am thrilled to find myself face-to-face with convolvulus flowers. I have never seen them before, but I know what they are because my favourite book is *The Book of the Flower Fairies* by Cicely M. Barker. From her painting I recognise the pink trumpet-shaped blooms, the trailing stems and the strange-shaped leaves. I want to know why these flowers don't grow near our home in Lancashire. I am beginning to notice that no two places are the same and I want to know what makes them different. I am also learning that books can teach me about the things I see.

On the other side of the path lies a field of white flowers. The air is perfumed with their scent and busy with bees. I don't know that these are broad bean plants. That knowledge comes years later when I grow them in my garden and breathe in the scent. It takes me back and brings the place to life as if I had seen it yesterday.

We are visiting friends in lowland Scotland. I am in a car, standing on the back seat with my head poking through the sunroof. We are speeding along a country road surrounded by fields of wheat, pale blue-green fields bright with scarlet poppies. This is a new experience. The fields I know in the Ribble valley are filled with grass and grazing cattle, or, up towards the moors, with rushes, calling curlews and sheep.

Now we are near Edinburgh. Rain is falling but we get out of the car to view the Forth Bridge. A train rumbles over but I am more interested in the water. Until now I have only seen the River Ribble and the tiny brooks that tumble down Pendle Hill. I want to know if this is the sea and am told that it's a mixture of sea and river. I am not satisfied. I want to see the real sea. We go to Portobello. I am enchanted and a life-long love affair begins.

At the age of five I have just started school in Clitheroe when we move house. The war is over, and my dad, newly released from the Air Ministry is to be Clerk of Works for a housing estate near Keighley. We are surrounded by machinery, noise and dust as new houses fill the fields on every side. There is only one place to escape. A patch of waste ground where houses have been demolished lies behind our garden. It is littered with rubble, and, to my delight, half hidden among tall grasses, there is an old tin bath. Surrounded by a sea of greenery that ripples in the wind like waves on the sea, this is my boat. Whenever I am missing, this is where they find me, sailing away on imaginary adventures fuelled by Robert Louis Stevenson's *A Child's Garden of Verses*.

Against the wall of a partially demolished house I find a small bush. Its leaves are soot-stained and its slender boughs are bent under the weight of tiny buds. My fingers are prickled as I pull it up, but I am undeterred. I take it home, plant it and watch with delight as the buds open into perfect white roses that fill the air with fragrance. I am given a copy of Frances Hodgson Burnett's *The Secret Garden*. I long to be Mary Lennox but have to content myself with a garden that can never be secret. I beg cuttings and tend my small patch with enthusiasm. I am a gardener with a place to make my own.

Two years later my dad trains to be a teacher. We have to quit the house because it is attached to his job. For a year he lives at the College. A neighbour's great-aunt offers the use of two rooms in her Victorian back-to-back house in Shipley. My mum, my sister and I move in. The only thing I insist on taking with me is my rose bush. We plant it in a pot and I clutch it all the way to 36 Field Street. I am excited. I expect fields, but I am bitterly disappointed. Row upon row of terraced houses stretch as far as I can see. There are no gardens. The only patch of green is the rosebush in its pot of earth.

The house is grim. We have stepped back a hundred years. The parlour, furnished by Aunt Elsie's grandparents, has never been updated. The chairs are stuffed with horsehair that prickles the backs of my bare legs. We spend most of our time in a scullery in the basement. It contains an ancient range that is spruced up on Fridays by the application of black lead. The shallow stone sink provides the only running water in the house. The toilet is outside. It backs on the street and we have to climb steps to reach it. Everyone knows where we are going — and why. We take a weekly trip to the Municipal Baths. The Superintendent is a tyrant who measures the depth of water and keeps a strict eye on the clock. She confiscates our bag of washing. After that we wear several layers of knickers and stuff our pockets with socks. We tip them into the used bath water and trample them with our feet. It's the only bit of fun we have. In summer it isn't a hardship, but in winter we step into cold streets, our hair still wet. We shiver all the way home, sleep in cold rooms, wake to windows iced with ferns and flowers that grow and blossom overnight.

I am six years old. For a whole week we escape the dreary routines of Field Street. We stay on a farm at Boggle Hole near the Yorkshire village of Robin Hood's Bay. I spend day after day on the shore. I search for fossils and explore rock pools. I get sand between my toes, paddle in the sea and jump the incoming waves. I cry when we leave. I want to live in Robin Hood's Bay.

I am nine years old when we return to Clitheroe. My rose bush, now in a larger pot, goes with me. This is my parents' hometown, but it never feels like home to me. The house is home, but there is something missing. We are forty miles from the sea and without a car of our own there are few opportunities to visit. Buses go to Blackpool, but to me it is a poor excuse for a sea. Promenades, piers and a sea that disappears into the distance at low tide have no meaning for me. I make do with the brook that runs near our house. I add stepping stones and build dams. I fish for bullheads and whiskers, marvelling at the way they camouflage themselves among pebbles and stones.

I get to know the limestone landscape of the valley and the contrasting millstone grit of the surrounding hills and fells. My dad enjoys walking and his interest and knowledge of wildlife is growing. Up into my teens, we walk for miles, often taking the bus to a starting point in the Trough of Bowland. I come to know the peat hags and open fells where black-headed gulls breed, the disused quarry where kestrels nest on a cliff ledge and the flooded pool where swallows skim the surface in search of flies. I tread upland fields and witness a lapwing feigning injury in order to draw me away from her nest. I find a little owl peering at me from a hole in an ash tree trunk. I walk the Hodder

Valley woods at bluebell time and find early purple orchids among the haze of fragrant blue. We sit in silence sharing sandwiches and I am breathless with excitement when a cuckoo lands on a nearby branch and sends out his echoing call.

I study Botany and Zoology at school. I am taught about the biological characteristics of species, but I am more interested in the relationships between plants, animals and their environment. I am fascinated by ecology before I ever hear the word. I go to Bingley Teacher Training College. The Biology Course is too book-based for me. I head for the Gardening Course and learn how to turn a patch of ground into a place that is filled with meaning. Only a fraction of what I learn is used in schools, but the rest informs my choices each time we move house. I can take a patch of earth and transform it into a place like no other.

I join a hiking club and a potholing club. A coach picks me up on Sunday mornings at nine o'clock and we head for the Yorkshire Dales. One weekend I am on the limestone pavement at the top of Malham Cove. I am learning about clints (blocks of limestone) and grykes (gaps between) that provide a micro-climate for plants that would otherwise be unable to flourish. The next weekend finds me beneath the bulk of Ingleborough, descending Bar Pot, crawling through mud, entering Gaping Gill where a 365 foot waterfall tumbles from above. I am told that York Minster would fit inside the main chamber. It is easy to believe. I feel very, very small. I am strapped into a chair and winched up through falling water. I reach daylight, drenched and dazzled. I sit on the grass, awed by what I have seen, aware of the weathering effects of water and of all that lies hidden beneath my feet.

I go on holiday to Skye. We stay in the Youth Hostel at Glen Brittle and I climb Sgùrr Alasdair, the highest peak of the Cuillins. This is scenery on an even larger scale. The peaks rise up, sharp-edged and bare. I climb on gabbro, a rough black rock that is nothing like limestone. I look down on a sea dotted with islands. I want to visit them all.

Panorama from the Summit of Sgùrr Alasdair.

Three thousand feet below, Glen Brittle's road
became a thread, the hostel miniaturised.

On either side the jagged peaks were magnified
by sunlight and rare clarity of air.

Loch Coruisk, a bowl of glassy blue
lay silent, mirror still.

Mountain Sorrel scraped a living
in cracks between frost-fractured rocks.

The great stone chute slipped to moorland
where bog asphodel bloomed profuse as buttercups.

But my eyes focussed on the west
to where a line of islands beckoned.

I marry, have children and devote myself to the busy life of a working mother. There are several house moves because of my husband's career. Each time we move, my rose bush goes with me. I take cuttings for my parents and my sister. For seven years I live in London. It is not to my taste. Everywhere is noise and bustle. The city is hot, the pavements hard and unforgiving. Lights are too bright at night. The Thames is hemmed in, dirty. Circumstances make it difficult to enjoy all that London has to offer. Sometimes I weep for the want of silence, for a cool breeze, for woods, moors, hills and the sea. I now know that place is of prime importance to me.

Each summer I take my daughters to my parents' house. Everything about the place is familiar. There is no sea, but after London, it almost feels like home. I relive my childhood as my dad introduces my girls to flowers, birds and insects. They do all the things I used to do. They feel the freedom of the fields, learn the names of plants, paddle in the river, watch dragonflies emerging from hard dark cases, their wings miraculously opening into flight.

London is stifling me. I have to leave. I go first to Northamptonshire. I forget my rose in the hurry to get away. I get cuttings from my sister, plant them and wait for them to flourish. We couldn't be farther from the sea, but there are woods on our doorstep and an active Naturalist's Trust. I re-engage with the natural world. I record all the plants in a nearby wood. I meet Richard and in 1976 we join a Botanical Society trip to Poland. Everything there is different. There are plants and butterflies I've never seen before. The foxgloves are yellow, the woodpeckers are black and we see a Camberwell Beauty. We climb Trzy Korony in the Pieniny National Park and look down on a medieval landscape. Strips of land are filled with contrasting crops, folk tend them by hand, travel by horse and cart, tether a cow or goat on every spare scrap of land. Houses are made of tree trunks slotted together, plaits of straw fill the gaps between.

A year later I return to Yorkshire. I do not forget my rose again. I am Deputy Head of a village school near York and we are within easy reach of the coast, the North York Moors and the Yorkshire Dales. Richard joins us and each weekend finds us out and about, getting to know the varied landscapes of this huge county. I revisit the Dales, and as I walk I recall the names of hills — Ingleborough, Whernside and Penyghent.

We visit Robin Hood's Bay. Although thirty years have passed, I find the farm where we stayed when I was six. We head for the village and I know there will be a jumble of narrow alleyways, that the houses will have red pantiled roofs, that swifts will be screaming and swerving between the chimney pots. I know that at the bottom of the slipway there will be sand and scars and sea.

I am forty years old and my life beside the sea begins. I am head teacher of a school in Scarborough. We explore the coast all the way from Spurn Point to Saltburn. We learn about seabirds at Bempton Cliffs and about chalk landscape at Flamborough Head. We search for jet at Whitby, but of all these places, Robin Hood's Bay remains my favourite. Five years later we find a house in the village. It is the realisation of a dream. We make what we believe to be our last move. On clear nights we walk on the seawall and admire the stars. I plant another garden where my white rose takes pride of place.

Friends invite us to join them for a holiday on Orkney. We walk round the Ring of Brodgar at midnight in June, crawl into Maeshowe and walk into Skara Brae before tourism demands entrance fees and restricts access. I love the wildness, the wind, the pounding seas, the signs of lives that lived here long ago. I find myself writing scraps of poetry, phrases about landscape, wildlife and history. My thoughts return to the day I climbed the Cuillins. Next time we take a holiday I will head for the islands of the west.

We travel from the Butt of Lewis down through Harris and the Uists to Barra. I feel an instant connection. I am standing on a deserted shore at Hushinish. The sea is aquamarine over near-white sand. The sky is clear and I am transported. What happens to me can only be described as an out of body experience. In the midst of this vastness I lose myself. When the sensation passes I am left with a lump in my throat and tears streaming down my cheeks. I am in love again, not just with sea, but with islands — with vast skies, bare rock, heather hills and shell-sand beaches. I am caught in a storm on the top of Chaipaval but am undeterred. It is wild, elemental, exciting.

Chaipaval

a day of sun —
views for miles around —

when suddenly
a shadow grows

and from across the sea
a storm blows in

a hammering of hail
that blocks the light

turns hill to white
sky to grey —

stranded on the summit
we huddle close

try to hide our faces
from the pelt

and when it passes by
we head for shore

find sea rocket blooms
leaf-deep in pearls

and milk-white hailstones
covering the sand.

We go home to Robin Hood's Bay. This most visited village in the North York Moors National Park is heaving with tourists. The beach is crowded. I miss the quiet of the Hebrides. I love the village at nights and in winter, but when the weather is good there is no peace to enjoy it. Every holiday finds us heading north, exploring the islands. They inspire me to read, write and take photographs. Going home to Yorkshire becomes harder after each trip. We wonder if it will ever be possible to live on an island.

In 1991, after a two and a half hour ferry journey we reach Colonsay. We find sandy beaches, seabird cliffs, hills that are not too onerous to climb, shingle, dunes, salt-marsh, bogs and lochs — all within eight miles by three. On the east coast there are woods of wind-stunted oaks. The grounds of Colonsay House are planted with exotic trees that merge into native species. Trees are scarce on islands so these are an added attraction; so too is the tidal island of Oronsay with the remains of a fourteenth century priory. We hear corncrakes, see chough and find the rare Irish ladies-tresses orchid. We stand beside an otter, asleep in a seaweed bed. Oblivious to our presence it sleeps on, only slipping away when the tide begins to rise.

The island school needs a head teacher. This is the chance we have been waiting for. Four months later we unload our belongings. Our island life has begun. We are part of a community of a hundred people and we get to know the island intimately. It is a place of contrasts. Winter nights are so dark that constellations are lost among multitudes of unnamed stars. The milky-way stretches like a highway across the sky. Summer days are long and the island is fragrant with wild flowers and the scent of Bog Myrtle.

Winds can be fierce. Sometimes we have to link arms to battle our way down the drive to the school bus, the smallest pupils tucked safely in between the bigger ones. Rain drives in from the west. In 1995 snow settles. Up to now my pupils have only seen a few stray flakes. We abandon conventional school in favour of snow. The children build their first snowman. We dance, make footprints, snowballs and snow angels. Their excitement is palpable.

I base most of our work on plants and animals, on landscape and on the history of this scrap of land surrounded by Atlantic Ocean. We sit in the woods at bluebell time and write about the sights, sounds and scents around us. We visit the graveyard, the beaches and the abandoned village. We cross to the skerries at the lowest spring tide to see what lies on the seabed.

The thrice-weekly ferry finds most islanders at the pier. It doesn't draw me. I like the isolation, being cut off from the rest of the world, the fact that the place itself is everything. After seven years I retire. Leaving is a wrench but we have to vacate the schoolhouse. Moving back to the mainland is unthinkable. We opt for Islay, buy a house with a garden that runs down to the shore and embark on a different style of island living. Islay is huge in comparison. With 250 kilometres of coastline and 3500 people we will never know it intimately, but I will have time to explore and even more time to visit other islands. I transform an acre of bracken into a wildflower garden. My Yorkshire rose is split and replanted. Soon I have three bushes flowering profusely from late May to mid July. They link me to all the places I've lived, to the five year old me planting my first garden.

I start to take writing seriously and almost everything that I write is based on place. I send illustrated articles to *The Scottish Islands Explorer Magazine*, and after a couple of years become a regular contributor. I describe the islands, seek out unusual aspects, write about things that a casual visitor might miss. I base other articles on specific themes— island trees, singing sands, plants of sandy beaches. Each one draws together my experiences on different islands. I write poetry too, aiming to capture the essence of each island that I visit. I attend Arvon Courses. I am encouraged to submit my poems, but realise that poetry magazines are like places. Each one is different and so I make a careful selection, subscribe, submit and am successful.

In 2009 I go to Tiree and find an old fence post that resembles a horse's head. Suddenly I am involved in make-believe. What if it is a real horse that has been bewitched? I weave the island's beaches, its Fairy Mound and Ringing Stone into an adventure story for 8-12 year olds. Nearly three years in the writing, *Cry at Midnight* was published by Cinnamon Press in 2014. It is Book One of *The Hagstone Chronicles*. Book Two was published in 2015 and Book Three will follow in 2016. Each one will be firmly rooted in the place that inspired it.

By 2010 I have visited all the inhabited islands of the Outer Hebrides, most of the Inner Hebrides and the Clyde islands. At this point I head for the Slate Islands. Here I find small islands characterised by black slate beaches and the remains of a once thriving slate industry. I have never seen anything like them and I am mesmerised. I sit on the tiny island of Easdale and write.

First Visit

Even on a sun-silvered day,
when this waste of slate
is dotted with heather
and the cliffs green with ivy,
there is melancholy here.
It floods my mind
the way the sea once topped
the quarry walls.
It tells of men who slaved
to split the slate,
women, children,
backs bent under waste,
trudging tracks
to tip it in the sea;
of wet winds blowing,
blowing from the west.

The poem tells a little of the location, the feelings the place evokes, something of the people and the history, but it is not enough. One poem cannot capture all that these islands hold. I want to delve deeper but I don't know why. There are more remote islands, wilder islands, more beautiful islands, but something grabs me and won't let go. I need to know more and write more. I gradually come to understand what is captivating me. Here are small communities, living in close proximity to signs and sights of the past. The history is inescapable, but nature is slowly and surely healing the scars.

Islands of Netherlorn

The islands are quiet now. Museums strive to keep memories alive, but no voice is left to tell the way it was. Yet stories speak in quarry walls, in flooded pools, in ruined powder stores, in rows of white-washed cottages, in beds of ancient slate:

Fields strewn with slate, tombstones carved from slate. Slate on cottage roofs, in harbour walls, in barriers built to try to stem the sea. Beaches heaped with slate. Waves turn and toss it, shift and sculpt it, but cannot wash it away, for these are the slate islands and slate will remain.

I collaborate with Jan Fortune. We plan a book — *Slate Voices: Cwmorthin and The Islands of Netherlorn.* The work occupies me for four years. During that time I spend seven weeks on the islands. I visit in every season for it is impossible to gain a true sense of the place when the sun is shining and the sea is calm. We set out for Belnahua when the sea is pounding. It is too rough to land but I feel the strength of the currents that run between the islands. They are powerful rivers, smooth-topped, pushing waves aside. I imagine what it was like to row two miles for barrels of fresh water and to carry the dead to Luing's Kirkyard.

Belnahua had no church, minister or burial place. I read a transcript of the gravestones on Luing. I find a child, Janet MacPhail who died on Belnahua at the age of eight. Her father's name appears on the carved slab, but there is no mention of her mother. I feel from a twenty-first century perspective. I am moved to write of the omission in her name. Perhaps I am wrong to do so. Back in 1840 it was probably the norm for women to be disregarded in this way. Rightly or wrongly, it brings me closer to the place than any of my other findings.

Catherine McPhail, Remembering 1840

I wrapped her in my shawl — my Sunday best,
no matter that I'll miss it when the wind
blows from the North with ice upon its breath.

I could not bear to cover up her face.
I held her tight and rocked her in my arms
and must have fainted then, for when I woke

she'd gone. Janet. I know I screamed her name,
not just my voice, but every part of me
called out and willed her back, alive and well.

I had to follow. Women held me back.
I struggled, fought them off, ran to the pier
to find the boat had left. My child had gone.

I could not see for tears but heard the plash
of oars grow faint, grow faint, grow fainter yet
until the sea had swallowed up the sound.

Imagined then, the things I'd never seen,
the jetty where they'd land, the coffin road,
the kirkyard and the lair. I could not bear

to think on that — her lying there alone.
I fell down on the slate, the cold, hard slate
and prayed and waited for my man's return.

He told me how he'd laid her in the lair,
and how he'd get a gravestone with her name
so her young life would never be forgot.

Now water lies between us, thoughts may cross
but all my words are scattered by the wind.
So here I sit on Belnahua's shore,

my eyes on Luing, my thoughts all filled with her.
He took me once, to show me where she lay,
to see the slate that marked her grave and name.

I saw the words. I read them all — and wept.

ERECTED
By..
John McPhail.
Belnahuay.
To. The. Memory.
of. His. Daughter:
Janet. Who. Depar
ted Thus. Life. SEP22
AGED. 8.YEAR MDCCCXL

I finally land on Belnahua, walk round twenty-seven acres dominated by quarries that have been flooded for a hundred years. I stand inside roofless cottages. The single rooms for one occupant are so small that my outstretched arms reach from wall to wall. I search censuses and birth certificates and populate the meagre two-roomed cottages with families long gone. I discover children who died between one census and the next. I read of a woman who spent sixty years on this tiny island. It is history, but it is not my history, yet I have delved so deeply into it that I feel connected to the place and all that has happened here. Fifteen pages of my poetry focus on this one tiny island. I didn't choose to write in such detail about this place. It chose me.

The deadline approaches. I could have gone on researching and writing, but it is time to stop. The book is published in May 2014. My writing has never been so deeply involved in a place, in its landscape, its history and its people.

Now I must find a new focus. I think about those writers who have influenced me in the past. Almost without exception their writing has brought places to life for me. The first time I go to Assynt I feel that I have been before. For that I have to thank Norman McCaig. Norman Nicholson's poetry evokes the same feelings about Millom and Black Combe, and although I cannot experience John Clare's 19th century

Northamptonshire, I see it clearly through the detail of his words.

For many writers and readers, this attention to detail is tedious. It can detract from the flow of a story, and sometimes writers add too much, almost as if they've spent hours researching and don't want to waste the facts they have discovered. I ponder on why some writers capture the essence of a place so vividly and so accurately that the reader is transported. I wonder why other writers add snippets that are so scant or inaccurate that a reader who knows the place is aware of discrepancies and misrepresentations. Such readers measure their knowledge against the written word, and where the two are in conflict, they flinch at the errors. For them, the writer loses credibility.

So what defines a place for me? In the first instance it is the landscape and the living organisms it supports. I am interested in why plants grow on limestone but not on millstone grit, why some favour moorlands while others prefer woodlands. These are things that are at the heart of my writing. They will bore many readers to tears, but I am not writing for them. I write in order to gain deeper insights into places and all they contain, and I write for people who appreciate the sincerity and accuracy of my work.

I am a naturalist and am disappointed that many naturalists dislike poetry. In 2009 I attended a lecture at the Linnaean Society. Following a reading of *Darwin's Microscope*, a poetry collection by Kelley Swain, a heated discussion pointed to the reason why so many scientists have no patience with poetry. Without exception, the criticisms revolved around inaccuracies. I side with the scientists. I am tired of glib references to wildlife, to swifts gathering on wires, to swallows screaming in flight, to plants growing in the wrong place and flowering at the wrong season. If authors wish to capture the essence of a place they need to observe it closely. Only then can they pick out the intrinsic qualities that make it different from every other place. Only then can they truly bring it to life.

I came across a paper, dated 1964, which features quotes from James Needham, the first Professor of Limnology at Cornell University. He drew parallels between botanists and poets. He described how both approach their work through study that leads to interpretation. The naturalist achieves his goal through homologies and intellect, while the poet expresses himself through analogies and emotions. Each, in his own way, formulates and delivers a message through patient and accurate observation. Poets who are good naturalists tell the truth without reverting to poetic licence to fit rhyme or rhythm. Naturalists who are good poets do the same. Good nature poems inspire the reader to observe closely in order to appreciate the experience that triggered the poem. While an observant naturalist who reads an accurate nature poem will see and appreciate the clarity of an experience that he has shared.

Of course, it all depends on whether or not place plays an important part in the piece of writing. For me, it is vital. It is the core of my writing, the starting point and the inspiration. It raises a multitude of questions. Why is this place as it is? Is it something about the weather or the quality of the underlying rock? Who came here and why? How have their activities changed the land? When I consider all these aspects it is obvious that they are interdependent. Then the fascination grows and I become involved in a deeper kind of searching as I try to connect with every aspect of the place.

I write about anything that catches my eye. I ponder on the qualities of individual species, rather like Gerard

Manley Hopkins in his belief that every living thing is characterised by a distinct and unique design that he called inscape. The Scottish poet, Kenneth Steven uses a similar word, wildscape. Birdwatchers have their own word — jizz, meaning a vibe, impression or unmistakeable characteristic through which one can identify a bird. I think these words can apply to places as well as to all forms of life. Whichever word one uses, this is what I am seeking. I have coined a word of my own and this will be the title of my next collection, due from Cinnamon Press in 2015 — *Waymarks*. Waymarks, in a conventional sense, are signs such as milestones and signposts. They are strategically placed to assist travellers to follow a route or reach a destination. In this poetry collection I give the word a broader meaning.

My waymarks are the milestones of my life — places, experiences and observations that have affected me in some way. Occasionally they lie dormant until something triggers a memory and brings them back to life. Others have had such a profound effect on me that I have immediately put pen to paper and preserved them in prose or poetry. Places can be anywhere and on any scale — a mountain top, a bluebell wood, a deserted beach. Some are recalled for their beauty — a landscape under snow, a waterfall, an island sky at night. Others are remembered as locations of holidays or because a particular plant or animal was seen there.

Some experiences are transitory and easily overlooked, but they show that something has happened in a particular place. They may be seed heads telling of earlier flowering, or empty nests suggesting that chicks have hatched. They may be even more fleeting, like an otter's trail that disappears when the tide comes in. There are intense observations too, things that pass without leaving a trace — the song of a bird, the flight of a butterfly, the glimpse of a deer in the undergrowth. Impossible to capture on camera they remain in the memory as clear as any photograph.

It is from waymarks such as these that my poems grow. Eventually I hope to have a collection of island poems. It will be called *From One Island to Another*. The title poem was written about the view of Ireland from my Islay home, but it applies equally to hundreds of views across The Hebrides:

From One Island to Another

Sometimes
there is nothing
to show there's land
across the sea.

When clouds convert to mist
that sits
on the sea's surface,
the mind relies on memory
to add the lines of islands,
the rise of distant hills.

When mist drifts and lifts,
the outlined islands,
shapes of distant hills
emerge like wraiths,
like shadows of themselves,
until sun scalpels through,
reveals each detail
sharp
against a blue so clear,
the miles of ocean
seem to disappear
and I could walk
across the water.

I have written many island poems, but there is always a longing to re-engage with the place in order to ensure that I'm happy with the image I've created. Sometimes a place eludes me and a poem is filed away for months, or even years. One such was *The Butt of Lewis*. I wanted to finish the poem but was unable to make a return visit. So I had to cast my mind back to 1988 when I made notes about the lighthouse, the vegetation and the birds. I looked at my photographs of buildings, cliffs and breaking waves. I re-read notes and found a draft poem in which I had selected the most striking images.

Although I had a list of plant species, I knew that the names alone could apply to many upland areas. So in order to create an image of a place where plants were stunted by the wind, I had described Yorkshire fog stems as bent, and heather as ground-hugging. Even so, my writing was largely descriptive. First-hand experience and detailed observation had failed to lift the poem off the page.

With the advance in technology I was able to search the web for information and images of the Butt of Lewis and its lighthouse. I found a blog that showed a feature that I had been unable to see. There had been a lighthouse Open Day and a visitor had posted photographs taken from inside the tower. Set in front of the light were two eagle owls made of stone.

I assumed that their purpose was to deter birds from flying into the light, but discovered that it was to discourage starlings from roosting on the dome and fouling it with their droppings. Including these facts added interest to my poem, but they needed to be related directly to the owls. Yet the owls knew nothing about them. From there, the first line virtually wrote itself.

The Butt of Lewis

Stone owls know nothing
of their lofty perch,
the red brick tower,
the warning light
that nightly cuts the dark,

— feel nothing
of the wild wind's chill,
drive of rain,
drench of salt spray
flung by storm-swept seas.

— see nothing
of the sheep-cropped grass,
bent stems of Yorkshire fog,
ground-hugging heather,
yellow hawkbit blooms,

jagged cliffs, each crevice
spilling campion and thrift,
tortured strata falling to the sea,
an offshore stack where shags
hang out their wings.

— hear nothing
of the pounding waves,
the drum of hail,
fulmars' cackling call,
cry of kittiwake.

Stone owls know nothing
of this starling roost,
storm petrels drawn to light,
small bodies smashed
from crashing into glass.

Whether or not it's a good poem, it provides several useful lessons. Never throw all your work away; at the very least, save notes and your best draft. Don't give in if something that initially inspired you fails to work. Read round the subject, think outside the box, find a different approach, tell it slant. Consider viewpoint. Experiences related through someone or something other than yourself can open up new possibilities, but if your aim is to capture the essence of a place there is no substitute for careful and prolonged observation.

The Place where we Meet
Jan Fortune

In 2012 the 'Writing Britain' exhibition at the British Library captivated me. There is something so powerful about an original manuscript or early proofs spattered with corrections; something intimate and epiphanic at once. All the books in the exhibition were united by a strong sense of place. I saw the hand-written last page of Stella Gibbons' *Cold Comfort Farm*, Alan Garner's *The Owl Service* (one of my favourite books from childhood and still one of the most powerful retellings of the Blodeuwedd story from the *Mabinogi*), a first edition of 'Little Gidding' — 'the end of all our exploring will be to arrive where we started' — and Kathleen Raine's Northumberland journals in her own hand, 'those abiding essences, the rocks and hills and mountains' raising their voices to 'utter their wild credo' next to a bit that reads like my own journal, talking about cold rural houses in winter with no central heating and managing the logs.

I came out awed, dazzled and dazed. I had entered a trance in there among runes and spells, within the song lines of connection. When I left, the world felt too bright and sharp. This is why we write — surely — for this extraordinary intimacy with strong magic, the reverie of words that make worlds. And in this enchantment, why is it that place features so dominantly? Why is it that in order to celebrate ten years of writing by hundreds of authors who have published with Cinnamon Press — poets, story-tellers, biographers — we have chosen to concentrate on the theme of place?

Because location — whether it is the 'nowhere' of utopia, the precise smells and sights of a Paris street, a

Welsh mountainside, an Indian market, or a Birmingham canal — and story are essentially linked. This is what the writers featured in the 'Writing Britain' exhibition knew. Writing takes us to a place – real and visceral, imagined and strange, dream or nightmare, anchored on a map or found only in the interior of a mind. Good writing takes us 'somewhere' even when the place is called 'nowhere.'

Because it is in a place that we begin to narrativise our lives, and the lives of our characters. We tell stories to reconcile ourselves to time — to the huge events of cosmology, to the big and small and hidden events of history and to our personal journeys — and in doing so we inevitably locate those stories — somewhere, someplace.

Because the most fundamental element of writing — language — is itself a place. Emil Cioran has an aphorism that we live in a language, not a place. I see this daily, living in a bilingual community and speaking only English (toddler Welsh not really counting). All of our experiences are filtered through language so my experience of 'home' (Tanygrisiau is a small village in North Wales) is different from that of neighbours, who were not only born locally, but speak a particular Welsh that is of this place, that mediates the place in a specific set of symbols. I also encounter this when I work with translators on a series of poetry anthologies for Italian minority language poets. Poets from Sardinia dream in one of ten languages, poets from Romangola in an array of dialects; the words they write give their experiences a particular texture and weight, affect their relationship to self, to others, to place. And I see this when I attend a launch in Paris with a bilingual audience and a book that is located on another continent, in Kanyakumari, India. Paris, a place I love, a place with powerful resonances for me and where I was recently engaged to my future husband, is not a monolithic location, but a place I know as a visitor, a place I access through my perspective, my history, my culture, my language. All of which makes the theme of 'place' endlessly variable, fascinating and fertile to writers.

For the last six years I have been writing about one tiny valley just above the village where I live. Cwmorthin is the most tranquil place imaginable; picturesque ruins lie around a lake in a hidden cwm at the foot of the Moelwyns in Gwynedd. In living memory it was still a working slate mine; go back a bit further and it was a Dantean hell, a cacophony of dust, noise, shouts, iron against stone. When I reach the top of the hill, I turn and look down over the ruins dotted around the lake. It is hard to imagine this place vibrating with the sounds of iron being hammered; trucks thudding along tracks; men shouting orders in the fast, guttural consonants of an endangered language; men coughing, each dust-filled heave tearing at their lungs; mules braying; the rhythmic chip and clink of slate being hewn or rived; the spray and hiss of water hosing down slate or churning in wheels; the occasional muffled boom of an explosion somewhere inside a tunnel. It is hard to imagine the smells: the sulphur-and-tar tang of coal burning, the gritty alkaline of dust and slate particles choking the air. It is hard to imagine the swell of activity in this place that was a little taste of hell, now transformed to a place of wild tranquility: uncompromising, raw, but beautiful.

There is no odour of industry, the air is cool and clean; the sharp iron tang of snow in the winter, the soft pungency of damp grasses for most of the year. The lake is quiet, an occasional lap of water on stone, but from here it gives back only silence. The sounds now are of an occasional bird calling, my own feet scrunching across the dry, springy heather, and the wind, which waxes and wanes in a fast repeating cycle; howling, keening, whistling before it suddenly falls away, exhausted and still. In those moments the hush spreads a blanket over the ruins: the barracks and lakeside workshop, roofless and fast becoming grim, eroded shapes of decay; the chapel, known as the sheepfold, its roof disappeared, its walls still reaching towards heaven in one last push.

Defoe, writing *A Journal Of the Plague Year*, sixty or seventy years after the event, spoke of how familiar places had been transformed beyond recognition by the ravages of plague, leaving a 'sense of haunted geography.' Slate mining had a similar effect. Tiny communities of farmers and small-scale non-commercial slate mining were overlaid by an industrial machine. The valley soon became unrecognizable and farming homesteads that had been in one place for centuries were obliterated in the name of progress. The process of transformation came again in less than a hundred years with the decline of the slate industry. Now Cwmorthin is home to neither farming nor industry, it's uninhabited; a place with a few ruins and a vast abandoned labyrinth of tunnels and chambers beneath the surface. Yet it is a place of haunted geography with a strong imaginative pull.

Most psycho-geography centres on the city, especially London and Paris, and psycho-geography that is sensitive to the history of place tends to be conservative; political commitment is sacrificed to historical tradition, to past resonances replayed. There is a similar tension in the psycho-geography of Cwmorthin, the tendency to hark back to a time of full employment, strong community, flourishing 'cabans', where men debated politics and religion in the language in which they also dreamt, can become deeply conservative. It can overlook the brutal working conditions, the deaths, the subservient relationships to mine owners and the narrow roles for women in an overwhelmingly male world. Ironically, such harking back and romanticisation is in deep contradiction to the spirit of debate and radical politics of the cabans themselves. That something is lost and gone does not mean it should be hallowed and sanctified. After all, the mine at Cwmorthin was known as the 'Slaughterhouse'. Yet there are also avant-garde and radical impulses within psycho-geography, characterised by writers like Blake, whose images are as transformative as they are apocalyptic, and who saw that rebuilding first requires destruction. Moreover harsh conditions invariably wake the human spirit to acts of resistance. 'Resistance is the secret of joy,' Alice Walker tells us in *Possessing the Secret of Joy*, her remarkable novel about, among other things, the horrors of female genital mutilation. Better to be nostalgic not for a life of grinding labour or the stench of toxic industry, but for a quality of engagement with life that Cwmorthin threw up despite the overwhelmingly harsh conditions. I'm interested in these contradictions and in these notions of transformation, defamiliarisation, engagement and reclamation made by the wanderer and poet; a collision of the political and the aesthetic; a collision of psychology and geography.

Of course, such collisions occur in many places. So why this particular place? It's a strange fascination. The disappeared lives in this now extraordinarily wild and tranquil valley were male, Victorian, Welsh-speaking. In short, a long way from the life of a Cambridge-educated feminist theologian, poet and editor who has struggled to progress beyond toddler Welsh for years. Yet the place simply wouldn't leave me alone. I'm

51

enthralled by the contradictions of a place that has gone from industrial hell to rural idyll, and also known loss through those changes, moving from a cauldron of debate, philosophy, religion and culture to emptiness. I'm intrigued by the parallels between the decline of the slate industry and the decline of the chemical industry on Teesside, where I grew up. And I'm mesmerised by the bleak, beautiful landscape with all the psycho-geographical possibilities it holds.

But beyond all of those rationalisations of why Cwmorthin spoke to me, why I spent six years of my writing life on it, is the simple fact that I happened to walk there during a snow storm at a point when my life was undergoing changes that seemed to me as cataclysmic as any metamorphosis of mudstone to slate or the transformation of industrial valley to abandoned ruins. And after that visit, I returned one February night, in torrential north-Welsh rain, when it was clear to me that the options in my own story were between revolution and breakdown. In short, I cared about the history of the place, I saw the parallels with other places I knew, and I found myriad resonances with this location because I was there, because I made an emotional link, because in trying to come to terms with my own narrative, this place played an enormous part. At the beginning of *Walden,* Thoreau says:

> I went to the woods because I wished to live deliberately, to front only the essential facts of life, and see if I could not learn what it had to teach, and not, when I came to die, discover that I had not lived. I did not wish to live what was not life, living is so dear...

> [Henry David Thoreau, *Walden*, Chapter 2]

There was a sense for me, as I walked up the long slate slope above Tanygrisiau and visited Cwmorthin over and over, that I was grappling with 'essential facts'. The abiding symbol for this, as I wrote an interlocked set of seven poetry sequences that became *Cwmorthin*, one half of the collaborative poetry collection, *Slate Voices* (written with Mavis Gulliver), was a building that I named 'Tŷ Schrödinger'. The name comes from a thought experiment devised by the scientist Erwin Schrödinger to illustrate a paradox in physics in which a (theoretical) cat in a sealed box may be both alive and dead. The little house was the only building not in a state of ruin. It was tiny, boarded, padlocked and sealed, and no-one could see into it. In my imagination it could contain both the past and the future. I had a constant longing to save this little cottage, and it became a symbol of mourning for a life-long and disintegrating marriage as the first roof tile fell away; knowing that inside the damp was winning, the stairs already rotten, that no-one would ever sit on the step for a moment of sunshine, watching the water play with stones on the shore, gaze up into the oddly out of place monkey-puzzle tree and think, *this is where I live:*

Tŷ Schrödinger I

The one remaining house is closed: windows boarded, padlocks guard the doors. Inside, unseen inhabitants, their lives already past, are yet alive and dead — until the seal gives way to break the spell. We know that they are gone, the dead, not smeared into some living-dying-life-inside-the-box; not caught between — but do not know the how or when the murk of maybes became death.

And in our box we wait until the measurement is made.

Another important symbol amongst the ruins around the lake was the Chapel, already in a state of advanced decay when I first visited Cwmorthin. In a former period of my life I had spent fourteen years in Anglican ministry. It ostensibly ended in three work place assaults, but the deeper story was the rupture with an institution of faith and my own metamorphosis, after a severe breakdown in health and almost sanity, to agnosticism. I wrote a litany for Cwmorthin that follows the days of Holy Week, leading up to crucifixion, but also with a sense of final hope:

Hallelujah

Long past Imbolc,
beneath a stick-thin tree:
a single snowdrop.

The first poem in the collection, in a series of short prose poems, signals that 'the path to the chapel is long' and that the building once known metaphorically as 'the Sheepfold' is now used as a sheep-pen was another metamorphosis that this valley enabled me to explore:

Cail

No hymns. Windows croon the strain of wind. Archways reach towards a glowering sky. No roof. No children chanting numbers, letters. No longer schoolhouse, chapel. *Cail*: the Sheepfold shelters animals now. Once these stones sang to praise a lamb slaughtered for their sake — *cigiddio*. No hymns. The moan of wind cries *marw* for the slaughtered; *marw, marw* through the broken arch.

Marw is Welsh for 'dead'. Margaret Atwood talks about writing as 'negotiating with the dead' and it seems to me that it is places with strong emotional resonances that facilitate this process of negotiation. It was in grappling with 'the facts' of life and death, of metamorphosis — geographical, industrial, emotional and spiritual — that this particular place became important to me. Knowing why a particular place calls to us gives the writing a place to dwell, and then comes the process. At Cwmorthin I was negotiating with the past of that particular valley, that particular slate mine, but I was also talking to my own dead – the death of faith; the death of a thirty-one year marriage begun at the age of eighteen. It was a powerful combination that found echoes in a powerful place and the image of the intact, but abandoned, house that gradually decayed persisted through the collection:

Tŷ Schrödinger IV

We tell stories because in the last analysis human lives need and merit being narrated ... The whole history of suffering cries out for vengeance and calls for narrative.

[*Paul Ricoeur,* Time and Narrative, Volume 1]

How this place honours ghosts,
how the long dead called me here
how mill house, engine, slate dust, noise
— are gone;
      how rain spears stone,

Tŷ Schrödinger is empty now,
an exodus Beneath the Steps,
abandoned homes.

How I came here
trailing broken wings,
shoulders rigid as faith;
how I healed
        and broke,

came to Cwmorthin in snow,
longed for this house
in its fold of slate.

How you left.

How Tŷ Schrödinger cracked —
the weight of years on stone
                          let go.

When I read the Cwmorthin pieces at the London launch of *Slate Voices* I was suddenly aware of how self-revealing they were. The place I'd written in, with its extraordinary rural and industrial history, its particular language and culture, had given me a story that had interwoven with my own and the result was a strange and powerful mixture that could only have arisen by encountering that specific place at that particular moment of my life. As I read extracts from 'A Litany for Cwmorthin' at the launch I was acutely aware of friends in the audience who had trained with me for Anglican ministry twenty years previously, one now a bishop, and of how our paths had diverged, partly as a result of the different places we'd ministered in. I was equally aware of how graciously they could enter into the place that Cwmorthin had brought me to. It was, for me, a place where a ruined faith could be laid to rest in peace:

Vigil

Wind desiccates tongues;

                                stay with me

slate dust chokes,

                             watch with me

we wait —

                               pray with me

What can we pray?

Have mercy?

Wind speaks in tongues

Eleison
Eleison
Eleison

Is silent now

Just say the word

But no Word comes.

Cwmorthin was also a place where I had gone for refuge and later to process the slow decay of a marriage that many friends later said was never meant to be. As I read poems which I had imagined were about a place and its history I was suddenly and overwhelmingly aware of how many people in the audience had seen me through some of the most volatile and dark moments of my life, not only in the move from faith to agnosticism via three assaults and ten years of extreme ill-health, but also in the dissolution of a marriage that had spanned the whole of my adult life. In his journal, Walt Whitman cautions, 'Understand that you can have in your writing no qualities which you do not honestly entertain in yourself.' This place that on the surface was of another culture, that was a mass of geological time and metamorphosis, that was seemingly so 'other', in fact had become deeply part of me; its metaphors mine, its qualities merged with my narrative. Writing about place isn't a matter of shifting the focus away from the personal, but a means of revelation, however elliptical. Like Thoreau, we go to particular places to live deliberately and in those places we find ourselves negotiating with the dead and constructing the future.

And so the Cwmorthin sequence ends at New Year, with a return to another place — the house I live in. This house, Tŷ Meirion, was my first refuge after the assaults that began my flight from ministry. It was the birthplace of Cinnamon Press and has nurtured this small shoe-string miracle of literary activism for a decade, making Cinnamon very much 'a place'. It provided the setting for my cross-over novel, *The Standing Ground*, about a post-dystopia Mabinogi-inspired Arthurian utopic community imaging a new future centred in Gwynedd. And it has continued to be a refuge as I construct another future in my personal life.

The last poem in the Cwmorthin sequence is 'Return to Tŷ Meirion':

Return to Tŷ Meirion

I want a house — secluded,
a place to keep the chaos
out, a granite womb:
slung against slate,
hills; the sound of birds
hurtling to stake their claims,
while wind intones its lullaby.

We become so used
to fractured days,
to weeks spent
keeping one step
ahead of the rains;

to months when all we can do
is mend the fence,
then mend the fence,
then mend the fence;

to endless years when
it is enough
to name the things
that anchor us —

this photograph
of a younger face,

this picture book
that I read to them

a thousand times,
this yellow shell,

this scrap of slate.

I want this place —
a foot on the crumbling earth.

Tŷ Meirion has been and is that place: for me, for my
family and for Cinnamon Press. Cinnamon is, amongst
other things, a place to stand; a space that allows for
multiple interpretations, by both writers and readers.

I'm currently working on a collaborative short story
collection with pieces from three writers. Adam Craig's
stories centre on Menton in the south of France;
character pieces, often approached sideways and with a
strong sense of place. Andrea Bianchi's pieces centre on
a childhood in Turin, often seen from a disconcerting
perspective. My stories are inter-textual in approach,
responding to both of these locales by threading
characters, scenes and verbal echoes from the Turin and
Menton stories into new pieces. In 'An Ordinary
Afternoon', the protagonist, Catherine, is an editor who
is reworking her own life as text, uncertain of what is
fiction and what is fact. She makes a journey from
Turin to Menton, then:

She heads along Avenue de Verdun, turns onto Rue
Partouneaux and Rue de la République, pauses
outside La Chapelle des Pénitents before ascending

the shallow steps of Rue de la Conception, the bells of the Basilique Saint Michel chiming the hour above her as she reaches the open doorway, narrow steps twisting up to the little flat.

At the door she flicks the pins of the key safe into combination, 1320, the number unchanged in four years. Inside everything is the same. The tiny kitchen leading into the living room, the same yellow bedspread draped across the futon against the far wall. There is a new cloth on the round table, dark red to match the plush of the chairs that stand by each long window, green shutters pulled in. The same rosé wine with a welcome postcard from Fenella stands propped between candles on the table. In the bedroom the white crocheted blanket drapes softly over crisp white sheets. She sits on the bed, looks towards the faded armchairs. She imagines him here with her; how he would write in the chair nearest the window, a wooden tray across his lap, bent over his work, blue eyes looking up occasionally.

She returns to the living room to unpack her suitcase into the curtained alcove filled with shelves and hanging space, useful boxes neatly labelled, 'light bulbs', 'shoe cleaning', 'ironing'…

This flat becomes a character, revealing features of those who inhabit it or interacting, even conflicting, with those staying there. Location is not incidental, but deeply telling, which brings me full circle: good writing takes us 'somewhere' even when the place is called 'nowhere'. It is in a place that we begin to narrativise our lives, and the lives of our characters, it is only in a place that I can meet you 'there'.

I am but mad north-north-west
Susan Richardson

'Feel free to pick up any artefacts that take your fancy,' says the cloaked and abundantly-bearded man standing next to the central fire pit. 'Try on a helmet. Ask me about this dragon's head I'm carving. Or how about you come on over and take a closer look at this sword?'

I shake my head, but since I'm sitting on a low wooden bench in the darkest corner of the longhouse, it's possible he doesn't notice.

'It's a fine sword — see?' The man picks it up and brandishes it in my direction. 'Nice and solid. Blade with a good wide blood groove. Come on — try it!'

I shake my head again, more vigorously and visibly this time. I want to stay sitting here, absorbing all the smells and sounds of this reconstructed Norse settlement, not be pestered into action by a posturing Viking.

'Got a busy day ahead of me, you know,' he continues in a voice as rough as the cloth of his dark red cloak. 'First I gotta order a few slaves around. Then I gotta check on the boat repairs and after that, I gotta go speak with Ragnar Red-Beard, the blacksmith, in his furnace hut. So why don't you come over and get a feel for this sword before I make a start?'

Look, you don't have to do all this re-enactment stuff for my benefit. It's not like there's a big tour group here that needs to be entertained for every second of its visit. There's just me, and I need peace to allow a full response to this place to rise, like the smoke would, if the fire were lit, through the hole in the turf-and-timber roof above.

'If you want to know how a sword like this is made, you should go speak with Ragnar Red-Beard too. He'll tell you how he collects bog ore from the banks along the brook and roasts it. Then he heats the furnace to 1200 degrees…'

I'm keen to learn about all the different activities that go on here, but eleventh century iron production isn't anywhere near the top of my list.

'…and once he's hammered out the impurities, there you have it — iron, ready to be forged into nails and other objects.' He gives the sword a flourish and takes a few steps across the dirt floor towards me. 'I'm Bjorn the Beautiful, by the way.'

Reluctantly, I get up off the bench and move to meet his outstretched hand. As I hold out mine, though, he deftly manoeuvres the handle of the sword into it. Victory sweeps across the parts of his face not masked by his beard. 'Get a good grip on it. Both hands if you need to. Heavy — yeah?'

It is, indeed, heavier than I would have expected or maybe I'm just not as strong as I thought. In any case, realising that I'm not going to get the peace I crave unless I fulfil Bjorn's re-enactment fantasies first, I start to waft the sword around a bit, trying to avoid bashing it against the assorted helmets and shields hanging from the wooden pillars that form a support for the roof.

'Now then, you got a score to settle with your neighbour, right? Or maybe there's a big blood feud going on, like in the sagas…'

Humouring him, I wave the sword a little more flamboyantly. I feel silly in the extreme though, illuminated as I now am in the column of light streaming in through the smoke hole in the roof. And of course it's just at this moment that the first few members of a tour group arrive, squeezing through the doorway, cameras already in point-and-shoot position.

The man who shoots first is wearing a too-tight sweatshirt with 'Save Water: Drink Beer' on the front and a badge informing us his name is Rick. Having captured a close-up of my ungainly sword-flailing, he lowers his camera and gives a blubber-lipped grin. 'Wrong sex for a Viking, aren't you?'

At this, I'm in danger of doing something untypically belligerent with the sword I'm still gripping in my right hand. I didn't come here for this. I haven't been on a momentous three-month quest through three different islands to deal with this sort of attitude at journey's end.

It's a quest that's taken me from the lava-strewn coast of Iceland to the southern fjords of Greenland and on to the Canadian province of Newfoundland, part of a wider region that was known as Vinland during the Viking era. For the last 430 kilometres I've travelled up Newfoundland's Great Northern Peninsula, with bleached pebble beaches and breaching whales to my left, and flat-topped mountains and tuckamore — stunted spruce and fir forests — to my right.

Twenty-five kilometres back, I checked into The Valhalla Lodge whose rooms are, I found, all named after Norse deities and saga characters, though I can't help thinking of mine not as Freydis' but as E. Annie Proulx's as it was the room where she wrote her celebrated novel, *The Shipping News*. Finally, for the last ten kilometres, I've travelled the road from Valhalla to this former Viking settlement, the UNESCO World Heritage Site of L'Anse aux Meadows. En route, I've glimpsed the sleek humped backs of yet more whales and, towering above even the plumes of mist from their blowholes, a solitary iceberg, a straggler, trailing down Iceberg Alley in the wake of the hundreds of others which must have studded the sea a few months earlier, in June.

Visiting L'Anse aux Meadows has been the ultimate goal of my journey all along. Here, some one thousand years ago, having sailed from the south-west coast of Greenland, a group of Vikings established the first — and only known — Norse settlement in North America. The setting has already fulfilled all my romantic land's end expectations — a serrated coastline of inlets, islets and crags and an agitated sea bleeding white-topped waves. As soon as I arrived, I was able to pick out both the reconstructed sod hut complex and the dips and ridges which mark the remains of the original excavated Norse settlement. Partly because I wanted to leave the best till last but mostly because the dips and ridges seemed to be infested by a large tour group, I decided to start by checking out the reconstructions.

I followed a boardwalk through tuckamore and across a boggier area brimming with edible berries. Another land's end attribute — a chill, skittish wind — made its presence felt and I zipped up my fleece and shoved my hands in my pockets as I crossed a creek and reached the first and largest of the four turf buildings.

I recognised it as a Viking longhouse with four interlinked rooms containing benches every bit as low as the sub-Arctic vegetation, a cooking area cluttered with pots and spoons, a space for weaving with an upright loom and colourful cloth hangings and, of course, the weapons/workshop room with the fire pit, Bjorn and his sword — and the wholly obnoxious Rick. He carries on grinning at me now, like he means to continue to taunt me, while I'm still poised to wield the sword at him.

Bjorn, to his credit, senses the tension and attempts to defuse it by switching into tour guide mode. All the other members of Rick's group have crowded into this section of the longhouse now too and Bjorn starts to rattle through a list of the food products which might typically be found in the adjacent cooking area.

'Fish, such as cod, that was left outside to dry. Partridgeberries and bakeapples. Butter…'

'Butter?' Rick's attention has successfully been shifted. 'There's butter here, you say?'

'Yeah, and other dairy products too.'

'Got cows here then?'

'Well — '

'Know for a fact there were cows in Vinland, do you?'

'No evidence has been found here at L'Anse aux Meadows, but at other Norse settlements, for sure…'

'Hah!' says Rick triumphantly like he's managed to catch Bjorn out.

In a peaceable, unstereotypically Viking way, Bjorn refuses to be goaded and goes on to talk about fishing methods instead. 'We Norsemen have a close relationship with the sea and fishing with nets and baited hooks is an important…'

'Fishing nets, eh?' As he speaks, Rick spits mist like a whale from its blowhole. 'Bet they didn't have the INTERnet back then though!' This is accompanied by a raucous guffaw which he clearly expects to be echoed by the rest of us.

'It's the men of the settlement who go out fishing of course,' Bjorn continues, showing more patience with Rick than I'd manage in a millennium. 'The women stay on land, preserving and preparing food and weaving cloth like this cloak I'm wearing…'

'Women? You're kidding me. Know that for a fact, do you? There were women in Vinland?'

I can stay silent no longer. Ice calves from my voice like a berg from a glacier. 'Oh yes, Rick. You bet there were women.'

*

I was teaching a literature course called Intrepid Women Travellers in the Centre for Lifelong Learning at Cardiff University when I was introduced to the extraordinary life of Gudrid-the-Viking for the first time. Though I'd expected to devote most of the course to the travels of audacious Victorians — to the ironic prose of Mary Kingsley in West Africa and what were deemed to be the indecorous adventures of Isabella Bird in the Rocky Mountains and beyond — my students were clamouring for more information about women travellers from the more distant past. A colleague pointed me towards two Icelandic sagas — *The Greenlanders' Saga* and *The Saga of Eirik the Red* — and promised that the woman that was depicted therein couldn't fail to captivate my students. I'd never really thought of myself as a saga sort of person, imagining blood-drenched raids by men with risible names like Harald Hairy-Legs and Magnus Flat-Nose, and an approach to travel that was wholly at odds with the peaceful, non-territorial women writers I'd read. I urgently needed some more early travellers to focus on though, so shoved my preconceptions to one side, got hold of copies of the relevant sagas and dived in. In the process, I took on board a whole cargo of discussions about their respective contradictions and inconsistencies, and gradually pieced together a composite picture of Gudrid's unconventional life.

She was born on the Snaefellsnes Peninsula in Iceland in the late tenth century, at the base of the ice-capped Snaefellsjökull volcano. As a young woman, she survived a perilous boat journey to Greenland — underwater volcano action caused volatile seas and many members of the crew perished — in order to farm and set up home in the Norse colony that had recently been founded there. Having outlived her first husband, she married Thorfinn Karselfni, an Icelandic merchant, and together, they organised and led an expedition to a land even further to the west, Vinland, where wild grapes were alleged to grow. The sea voyage this time was much calmer, which was just as well, as Gudrid was most likely pregnant at the time, giving birth some months into the settlement period to the first European in North America, a son, named Snorri. She and Karlsefni and their crew lived and adventured in Vinland for about three years, before moving back to Iceland, where she gave birth to another son and settled on a farm in the north-central region of the country. After Karlsefni died, although her days as a wife were over, her days as a traveller certainly were not, as she embarked on a pilgrimage to Rome. The continental plates of paganism and Christianity seem to have shifted and collided inside the young Gudrid but by her later years, her conversion was apparently complete.

I drank in her story with the pleasure of a Greenlander guzzling the first wine from Vinland grapes, and found myself craving more. I raided libraries and scrolled through the catalogues of online bookstores, seeking any book that was even vaguely connected with Gudrid's travels: since I found only two, I broadened my search to include Viking life, other Icelandic sagas and, finally, and most wholeheartedly, the countries where she settled. I invested in a glossy, large-scale atlas that devoted a double page to Iceland instead of adding it as an afterthought to the upper left corner of Europe. I located the Snaefellsnes Peninsula, a misshapen arthritic finger reaching into the North Atlantic, and I pored over a map of the whole of Greenland too, so immense compared with the lopped-off version more commonly seen on maps of the world.

Over the next couple of months, in fact, I spent every spare waking moment absorbing as much as I could about the countries that had formed and fortified Gudrid, while at night, my need to absorb yet more would wake me with its screaming, demanding to be fed. Finally, when Lonely Planet guides to Iceland, Greenland and Atlantic Canada took up residence on my desk, I realised the research I was doing went way beyond Intrepid Women Travellers teaching preparation. Somehow, at some point, I seemed to have alighted on the idea of going travelling — and writing about the experience — myself.

There followed a year of intensive journey-planning, alongside seeking and securing sufficient funding, during which time my writing intentions came into clearer focus. I resolved to produce a prose narrative, one that blended an account of my own explorations with Gudrid's from a millennium before, and I also aimed to integrate themes of migration and the status of women in both Gudrid's era and the first decade of the twenty-first century in each of the countries I visited. To that end, I set up numerous interviews en route — with the Director of the Library of Women's History in Reykjavik, with the founders of the Feminist Association of Iceland and with the President of the Provincial Advisory Council for the Status of Women in St. John's, Newfoundland, to name but a few. All were, without exception, engaging and eloquent interviewees who gave me invaluable insights into the history and gender politics of their respective countries. As I travelled, however, it was the landscape — and my evolving relationship with it — that continued to obsess me more than anything else.

Initially, in spite of all my pre-trip reading and research, Iceland, with its lava fields, volcanoes, seething mud pots and sulphur-streaked fissures, seemed like a strange and impenetrable new language in which I was suddenly taking an intensive immersion course. 'To my right, the striped strata of rhyolite mountains, unrecognisable dialect of lilac, pink, gold,' I scribbled in my notebook, shortly after setting out on a three-day hike in nagging rain. 'Below is the sandur, embroidered with braided rivers. I stumble past the tongue of the glacier, with its mumbles of crevasses and moraines, then struggle on towards the waterfall, where basalt pillars baffle like inflected nouns. Yet as I speak its name aloud — Svartifoss…Black Falls…*svart*…swarthy — I start to understand the language of this landscape, and bubble with lava joy.' Though this description feels forced and mannered to me now, I remember scrawling it quickly and urgently as the rain fell, not as a prose paragraph, but with line breaks in couplet form.

Day by day, hike by hike, the landscape proceeded to shift me ever more towards poetry. Metaphors and similes erupted onto the pages of the notes I was making. Prose, conventional sentence structures and paragraphs couldn't contain it somehow.

One month on, by the time I'd made it to the north-central part of the country where Gudrid spent her final years, something else had dawned on me too — after my initial sense of dislocation, the outer landscape through which I was travelling was, for the first time in my life, matching my inner landscape, complementing my emotional topography. As an only child who had always craved solitude, huge horizons and sparse populations, I'd never felt more at home.

In Greenland, my relationship with the landscape evolved into another phase. After being led by a guide on a challenging hike to a spur of the inland ice cap, and both hearing about, and seeing for myself, the rapidity with which the ice was melting, I could no longer relate to the environment in the same way. As I crawled into a dripping ice cave at the front of the glacier, the roof and rear wall of which were the deepest and most intense blue I'd ever seen, I realised that though the landscape had afforded me the opportunity to enjoy some epiphanic travel experiences and to satisfy my self-aborbed quest for outer tranquility and inner peace, this was no longer enough. The Arctic and sub-Arctic were far from being one of the last untouched wildernesses left on earth: though vast and little-populated, this environment was suffering irreparable damage from the impact of human activity elsewhere in the globe, with galloping climate change just one of the consequences. As I continued to travel, question, listen and discuss, I was made increasingly aware of the spectres of species-level extinction, resource depletion, and organochlorine pollution throughout the oceanic food chain as a result of our profligate pesticide use. To move through the landscape — be it on foot, by bus, boat or small plane — without being mindful of its increasing fragility and vulnerability, was now inconceivable.

As a result of all these shifts in perspective, by the time I returned home to the UK after the climax of my journey in L'Anse aux Meadows, I was no longer intent on writing a prose narrative; indeed, many of the poems that form the first section of *Creatures of the Intertidal Zone* (2007) were already well underway. Gudrid remained central to my vision and a sequence in her voice, each poem relating to a different landscape and distinctive period in her life, opens the collection. I was still interested in the theme of migration too, but having spent several days near Gudrid's birthplace on the Snaefellsnes Peninsula observing a breeding colony of Arctic terns, a bird that has one of the longest known annual migrations, from the Arctic to the Antarctic and back again, the journeys of non-human animals were now as fascinating to me as anthropocentric ones.

As I continued to write, I plunged into a period of reading and research again and discovered a book that remains on my Top Ten List of All-time Favourites — Barry Lopez's *Arctic Dreams*, a celebration, in poetic prose, of the Far North and those who inhabit it, an overview of its history and likely future, and an exploration of the link between landscape and imagination. The Arctic tern tugged me south to the Antarctic, too, and as well as reading more widely about the impact of climate change and starting to school myself in the rich vocabulary of ice, I also ploughed through countless late nineteenth/early twentieth century South Polar explorers' narratives. *Terra Incognita*, travel writer and biographer Sara Wheeler's engaging 1990s account of her months in Antarctica researching and writing alongside groups of polar scientists also attracted me, and I pondered long on her depiction of the ice as a 'perfect *tabula rasa*' onto which one's own personal preoccupations and obsessions can be projected.

It was at this point, too, that the icescape started to enter my dreams. Over a period of about two months, that most iconic of Antarctican creatures, the Emperor Penguin, made a series of surreal appearances — and on each occasion, towards the end of the dream, I bizarrely found myself metamorphosing, feather by feather, flipper by flipper, into an Emperor Penguin myself. These dreams were so repetitive, so vivid and visceral that it was only a matter of time before the penguin, as symbol and metaphor, moved out of my dream-landscape and began to feature in the poems that make up the final two sections of *Creatures of the Intertidal Zone* too.

After the publication of this, my first full-length collection of poetry, I thought I'd probably written all I'd ever want, or was able, to say about the sub-Arctic, Arctic and Antarctic regions, but polar poems kept emerging. I also happened to meet a visual artist, Pat Gregory, at around the same time — I'd seen several of her linocut prints in the annual Wales Artist of the Year exhibition and we quickly discovered that we shared both a mutual appreciation of each other's work and an abiding interest in the Far North. After several long, impassioned conversations, we decided to try to embark on a collaboration, working towards both a touring exhibition and a joint collection of poetry and prints. In addition to drawing on memories of our own travels, we promptly delved into Inuit folktales and also spent many an hour discussing another much-loved book, *The Idea of North* by Peter Davison, which looks at the representation of North in different mythologies, landscape art and literature, and also analyses how that particular point of the compass, and the way in which we orientate ourselves to it, has very different resonance for different geographies and cultures.

As we outlined in the introduction to our joint collection, *Where the Air is Rarefied*, which was ultimately published by Cinnamon Press in 2011, the collaboration encouraged us to move in creative directions that we would never have taken had we not had the constant stimulation of each other's discipline. Gradually, out of our many discussions, a succession of paired poems and prints came into being: we didn't want the prints simply to illustrate the poems, however. Instead, our intention was that both genres would engage with a specific North-focused theme — be it environmental, socio-cultural or character-driven — and evolve concurrently. We then moved on to creating a stepped series of works over a period of several months in which one of Pat's prints, produced in response to one of my poems, triggered the next poem in the sequence and so on, resulting in a total of nine new pieces.

Pat and I indulged our shared fascination with the landscape of ice too. Against a backdrop of distressing predictions suggesting that the Arctic would soon be entirely free of ice during the summer months, we grappled with the subject of human-induced climate change and its impact on the North, and explored ways in which we might express this through visual art and poetry. In spite of relishing the language of ice — frazil, vuggy ice, growlers, bergy bits, tabular bergs, nilas — I realised that one of my ongoing challenges would be finding innovative ways in which, and different angles from which, to write about it. Eventually, after I'd experimented with, and rejected, a range of different forms, our 'Tip of the Icetongue' sequence resulted, with my fragmented poem-footnotes referencing Pat's series of ice-melt prints. My poems grew consistently more fragmented and minimalist, in fact, as our collaboration continued, a development that was as exciting as it was unexpected.

In addition to focusing on ice's propensity to shapeshift to liquid from solid, we became fascinated by metamorphosis of another kind. In the context of Inuit folktales, shapeshifting from human to non-human animal or even to an apparently inanimate object, is often a means by which characters negotiate, and manage to thrive within, the landscape. Young girls, for example, change into ravens or ptarmigan and rise above their ice-bound communities to escape the advances of unwelcome suitors. A resourceful grandmother converts her own vagina into a sledge so that she can head off and hunt her own food without having to rely on her neglectful family. And in one creation tale, versions of which are found in both Arctic Greenland and Canada, a girl who ultimately takes up residence on the ocean floor as Goddess of the Sea has her fingers and thumbs chopped off by her father. Her amputated digits transform into the creatures of the deep — the world's first whales, narwhals, seals and walrus — and she thenceforth has the power to decide if humans have earned the right to a successful marine mammal hunting season or whether they've been ill-behaved and caused damage to the environment and therefore deserve to starve.

These creative and dynamic responses to the Far Northern landscape on the part of the region's indigenous inhabitants, as represented in the folktales, are, we discovered, in stark contrast to the way in which the environment is portrayed in many nineteenth century accounts by European adventurers. Often ill-equipped, and sticking resolutely to their European diet and clothing instead of learning survival skills from the Inuit, those who ventured to the Far North viewed the landscape as unremittingly hostile, yet persisted in seeking to dominate, rather than negotiate their way through, it. There is evidence of gender stereotyping too: in both written accounts and a contemporary 'Punch' cartoon, the Pole is portrayed as a woman waiting to be won, a virgin icescape anticipating penetration by a rugged male explorer. Conversely, Pat and I also came across some personifications of the North as male (cold, rational, emotionless) and the South as female (warm, irrational, passionate), and gained much pleasure from subverting these gendered conventions in several of our poems and prints.

*

From being sparked by Pat's visual art to envisioning the North through myth, imagination and memory, writing place-based poems in *Where the Air is Rarefied* was a process to relish. Yet since that time, my relationship with landscape and the way in which I choose to write about it, is evolving again.

After feeling itinerant and restless for much of my twenties and thirties, living overseas for a number of years and then travelling in, and focusing exclusively on, the Far North, I have since sought to become more rooted, and this has taken the form of getting to know Wales, the country where I was born but from which I moved at the age of eighteen, on a deeper level. Though I grew to love the Arctic and sub-Arctic with a passion, I couldn't shake off the feeling that I was always likely to remain a visitor, passing through the landscape rather than being a product, and an integral part, of it. When I sailed, for example, among mostly-submerged icebergs in a tiny, lurching boat in thickening mist off the east coast of Greenland, I spent the entire journey clinging to the prow and suppressing a shriek whenever it bashed into a barely-visible berg and pitched to one side, causing my gloved hands to plunge into the freezing water. The Inuit boatman, meanwhile, who'd been dealing with similar conditions all his life, was imperturbable, and I realised I'd probably never reach the point when such an experience would feel anything but alien and disconcerting.

Reconnecting with Wales, or one particular corner of it at least, has, so far, been a fruitful and joyous practice. I now spend as much time in Pembrokeshire as possible and walk the coast path daily, writing detailed journal entries about the first appearance of spring squill, thrift, and kidney vetch; the births, sucklings, moults and storm-spawned deaths on the grey seal pupping beaches; the flight paths of red kites and kestrels. I undertake volunteer sea watches, spotting harbour porpoises, bottlenose and Risso's dolphins from cliff tops along the coast, familiarising myself with sea state, wind direction and tidal turnings. I sow wildflower seeds for bumblebees and butterflies, and vegetable seeds galore. I grow potatoes, courgettes, pumpkins, butternut squash, sweetcorn, beetroot, carrots, parsnips — literally putting down roots and getting to know my small patch of earth more intimately by digging it, smelling it, burying my hands in it, wrist-deep. Through the annual growing cycle, I'm slowly learning which vegetables won't fare so well and which are likely to thrive.

As time goes on, I'm increasingly understanding, in an embodied, experiential way, what I've long understood, fuelled by years of reading deep ecology theory, on a more cerebral level — that I'm just one part of the environment in which I've based myself, one part of the more-than-human world, one part of an interconnected web of beings.

As an extension of this understanding, I enjoy facilitating Wild Writing Workshops which aim to encourage participants to engage with the natural environment, and re-imagine their place in it, through the writing of poetry and prose. These workshops, which can be as short as a morning or as long as a six-day residential, include both outdoor elements (such as guided walks, with writing prompts) and indoor writing and sharing sessions. One of the prompts to which participants respond most enthusiastically, and which seems to trigger the most startling pieces of writing, draws on the work of philosopher and cultural ecologist, David Abram.

In his acclaimed work of ecological philosophy, *The Spell of the Sensuous*, Abram asserts that 'To touch the coarse skin of a tree is to experience one's own tactility, to feel oneself touched by the tree. And to see the world is also to experience oneself as visible, to feel oneself seen.'

I like to allow at least an hour — ideally, much longer — for workshop participants to explore the landscape in which they find themselves, and through which they're moving, with this quote in mind. I urge them to experiment with tactility, in particular — to take off shoes and socks and encounter the touch of the earth with bare feet, to lean against trees, to stand still with eyes closed for a while, to lie down...

How does it feel, I ask them to contemplate, to alter their perspective in this way, to experience being seen and touched by an animate landscape, to consider themselves as acted upon instead of always being the agents, the ones doing all the touching and seeing? And how does this feeling impact on their writing, both in terms of content and the way in which words fall onto the page?

It can be useful to try this exercise in different environments, at contrasting times of the day and/or night, in different seasons and in various weather conditions. After exploring the landscape through the body, free-writing and gathering as many impressions as possible, some participants like to use their notes to craft a place-infused poem or piece of prose while still outside, whereas others prefer to retreat, reflect and write indoors. Again, it's useful to try both options and consider which of the resulting pieces of writing seems to have the most resonance.

Another means by which I'm striving to reconnect with, and write directly from, my native land is through immersing myself in folktales. Having been so stimulated in the past by myths and legends from other cultures, including Inuit and Norse, it's been instructive to rediscover, or come upon for the first time, stories from the Welsh tradition. One of my ongoing fascinations is the medieval tale of the sorceress, Ceridwen, and her servant-boy, Gwion Bach. After concocting a wisdom-bestowing brew intended for her son, Ceridwen instructs Gwion Bach to keep stirring, for a year and a day, her cauldron of *awen* (inspiration). However, having accidentally sampled a few drops of the potion and realising that he will incur her wrath, he takes flight and proceeds to move through an exhilarating series of incarnations, from hare to fish to bird to grain of corn, while Ceridwen pursues him as greyhound, otter, hawk and grain-eating hen. Finally, as a consequence of swallowing Gwion in his corn form, Ceridwen becomes pregnant and gives birth to Taliesin, the bard.

Aspects of this multi-textured tale are currently permeating my poetry in a range of different ways. The Gwion Bach side of the story features in a sequence in my recently-published Cinnamon Press collection, *skindancing* (2015); Ceridwen's voice, however — inspired, in part, by the idiomatic Wenglish of my maternal grandmother — remains a work-in-progress. In the following extract, my aim is to allow the landscape to be present in two contrasting layers. Though Ceridwen has shapeshifted into a dog at this point, her human, cognitive mind is still to the fore, and the suggestion of a locale emerges through her use of herb-related imagery. A different version of the same location, plus an impression of her movement through it, is simultaneously evident in the more sensory, italicised doggish sections. I also want to convey the feel of a changing environment, one that's different from when Ceridwen was a child, as a result of anthropogenic climate change. Though it's not yet on the scale of the melting of Arctic ice and there's only a hint — a reference to 'awful storms' and a fallen tree — in the excerpt that follows, it's certainly something to which I intend to return as I continue to develop the piece and move Ceridwen through her succession of animal selves.

I've also come to realise that the spirit of Gudrid is somehow present here too. Though Ceridwen doesn't, of course, sail in turbulent seas from Northern isle to Northern isle, she is still, in her own way, an intrepid woman traveller in that she gamely and tenaciously journeys from skin to skin. Landscape in this piece is, I think, going to be as much about the landscape of the body as it is about the external environment.

And it's going to be about the landscape of the shapeshifting text, too — a text that's not quite a poem, not quite prose and not a straight dramatic monologue. A text that's also on a journey, restlessly seeking its final form:

Hark at me, creaking.
Quick as chickweed I'd've been, not so long back.
Brand-new rig-out just like this one —
fur, four legs, the lot — then off over the hills,
no sign of cramp or rheumatics.

(sniff   sniffupridge sniff
sniffoverroots sniffsniff
sniffsniffsniffsniff gorsegrass sniff grassgorse)

Speed isn't everything, mind.

(loop sniff backtrack mmmm sheepy here
solidsmells on breeze mmm sniff squat pisssssss)

He'll run out of puff soon enough,
or stop to eat or sleep for a spell.
If he thinks he can get away with doing what he's done
just 'cause he's learnt to put a spurt on —
well, I'll show him, plain as cowbane.

(up mudgrass upup sniffsniff
sheepshit! sheepshit! sheepshit! licklips lipslick)

Boiled up that broth special for our Morfran, I did.
Can't let on what's in it,
but it would've altered him beyond.

(sniff sniff   roll in it roll   sheepshitty me
lolltongue lolltongue thirsty)

And it's not got any of the muck

(smellwater mudpuddle)

they put in the shop-bought stuff.

(laplaplaplaplaplaplaplaplaplap)

Anyhow, I left that Gwion Bach
in charge of the stirring.

(laplaplaplaplaplaplaplaplaplap)

'Go steady now — don't rush it,' I tell him.
'A twelvemonth and a day that's got to cook for.

(laplaplap)

And don't even think of having a taste of it

(lap)

or I'll be mad as yarrow.'

(down mudgrass sniff down down
grass   othershit rabbit   downmud downdown sniffsniff
sniffsniffsniffsniffsniff Him! Him! Him!)

Well, he can't be far off now.
(Him! Him! Him! Him!)

See that poor old birch tree over by there by the river?
It must've come down
in one of the awful storms we've had.

(Him!)

And d'you know what I reckon?
He's cwtched in under the roots.

(growlmouth)

(not a tailwag face)

I'll have him now in a minute.

Paris, India and The Quest for the Big Orange Poetry Flower
Hazel Manuel

Slowly parting lips…I can think of few more sensual sights, especially in the half-light of a wine-soaked Saturday evening. The twin candlelight cones that flickered in Christophe's eyes suggested mischief, as two slender fingers and a thumb stroked the stubble on his chin. Natalie was watching him too, her own fingers by her shoulder clasping a half-spent cigarette, a coil of smoke rising into the haze above the table. I breathed deeply its scent which mingled with her musky perfume, and closed my eyes as a bare foot brushed against my un-stockinged leg — Fabian's? For a moment, in spite of the babble of voices and the wind battering rain against the window, only this and Jacques Brel's exquisite refrain existed… '…*ne me quitte pas…*'

'I have been thinking about something.' Christophe's French accent emphasised each syllable and he turned towards the bookshelves behind him, indicating with a flourish the rows of shadowy tomes bearing witness from their wooden shelves.

'Is a sense of place important in literature?' The question was thrown down like a gauntlet and Christophe reached for the wine bottle amidst the debris of the meal. 'Does a novel actually need a sense of place at all? Do you not think that a strong plot, a competent narrative and engaging characters can be enough?' He filled his glass with what remained of the Pomerol and, locking his eyes on mine, licked a droplet from the crystal lip.

'It's an intriguing point,' I said. '*Huis Clos* could be an example?' I retrieved the third bottle, as yet unopened and passed it to Fabian who winked at me and rummaged among the napkins and used plates for the cork-screw.

Natalie tilted her head toward the ceiling and we all watched her blow a long translucent tendril from between her lips. '*Oui*' she said, the smoke continuing to escape the corners of her mouth, 'but *Huis Clos*, it is a play *n'est-ce pas*? That is different.' I enjoyed the way she made '*it is*' sound like '*tease*'. She narrowed her eyes as Fabian stood to wind the screw into the squeaking cork. 'If we include plays though,' she continued, 'I imagine Sartre thought that not having a defined place left him freer to focus on exploring his ideas.' The bottle opened with a satisfying *pop!*

'Exactly,' I said, holding out my glass to Fabian. I put my nose as far into it as it would go and took a deep sniff. 'Cherry chocolate,' I said. A staccato siren blared up through the wind from the street below but no one took any notice. Natalie turned to me, her elbows still propped on the wine-stained table cloth. Her ruby ring flashed red-gold in the candle-light. 'Sartre wasn't distracted by the need to create and sustain a setting,' I continued. 'In *Huis Clos*, there is no '*place*' as such, only characters in a room, so as Natalie said, what is foremost for the audience are the ideas that Sartre is inviting us to explore.'

The wind threw a sheet of rain against the window, making the panes rattle in their frames and the candles gutter. '*Le temps est terrible*', Natalie muttered, flicking her lighter two, three times and putting the flame to another cigarette. I savoured the pleasantly acrid smell of the smoke she blew across the table as the foot against my leg crept higher.

'*C'est vrai, vous avez raison*,' Christophe said. 'If the themes in the piece are universal and the writing strong enough, then the piece will stand alone.'

'Okay, but consider this,' I said. All eyes turned once more to me and I watched the candle-light sculpt deep shadows into Christophe's cheeks. 'I suggest that even if the place is undefined, or is an unspecified 'every-place' it will still evoke a sense of the *kind* of place it is.' Christophe locked eyes with me over the top of his glass. 'Think about *The Road*', I said. 'We never learn where the novel is set, but McCarthy continually reminds us of the bleakness of the landscape, and a large part of the novel is an exploration of the characters' relationship with it so that we really feel like we are there, trying to survive in a post-apocalyptic world.'

'*Pah!*' Christophe exclaimed. The toe stopped caressing my leg.

A smile played around the corners of Fabian's lips. Jacques Brel was imploring us to '*love what must be loved and forget what must be forgotten*' and I took a long, slow sip of wine.

'*C'est vrai,*' Natalie said. 'Kafka's *The Trial* is similar, *n'est-ce pas*? It doesn't matter that we don't know where the novel is set, only that it takes place in some oppressive régime.' I watched the tip of her cigarette glow red as a finger of ash lengthened and dropped to her plate. 'A '*place out-of-place.*' It creates the synergy between the narrative and its setting, *non*?'

'Okay then,' Christophe said. 'It's the same with *Huis Clos*. Here we learn nothing about what or where this room is. The whole piece relies on the dynamics between the characters and as such the lack of a sense of place emphasises the tension Sartre creates between them. A place that we can name and recognise — an actual place that exists somewhere in space and in time is not necessary. '

'*Tout à fait!*' Natalie flicked more ash onto her plate. '*Mais*, most novels are not like *The Trial* or *Huis Clos*.

Kafka and Sartre achieved something unusual. And they went further than McCarthy, in *The Road*. *Non*, c*'est pas normal*. Most of the time we know where a novel is set…' She held up a hand to silence a barrage of interruptions. '… Or at least what the setting could feasibly be. One could argue that the location is a part of what makes the novel interesting, *n'est-ce pas*? *Mais…*' She looked around the table and I followed her eyes, watching the candle-light carve each face into a pared-back version of itself. 'That doesn't make a sense of place *necessary*, only *sufficient*.'

'I see it differently.' We all turned to look at Fabian. He reached across Natalie and ripped a piece of bread from the half-eaten baguette and we watched as he picked up Christophe's knife and gouged out a hunk of almost liquid Camembert. I imagined the faintly ammoniac taste of the dripping cheese as he continued:

'Christophe has stated that a strong plot, a competent narrative and engaging characters can be enough. I ask you now, why should we be content with '*enough*'? Regardless of the philosophical distinction of what is necessary and what is sufficient, and irrespective of what the setting is or isn't, surely it is simply better for the authenticity, indeed for the integrity of a novel for it to present a strong sense of place, whether real or imagined?'

An explosion of French and English animated the table as we all spoke together. Christophe waved his glass in front of him insisting '*la distinction est indispensable!*' Natalie blew smoke around the table, repeating '*mais non! Mais non! C'est trop facile!*' 'Can't ideas devoid of context be meaningful?' I asked, projecting my voice into the din.

Fabian looked around the table, his eyes engaging ours in turn. Christophe's face had frozen into a bony grimace of shadow and light, his hands stretched before him as though in supplication. Natalie was holding her cigarette above her head in mid-flourish, her other hand flung out to one side, her wine glass having sloshed its contents onto her cheese. My eyes came to rest on Fabian's lips which curled into a smile. The toe returned and began moving up my leg.

Fabian smiled at the passion he had roused. '*Mais oui,*' he replied, the Parisian '*eessh*' sound laying emphasis to his conviction. 'Regardless of Sartre and Kafka, and of the purity of ideas, my belief is that setting a novel in an actual, identifiable place is a powerful way to lend credibility to a narrative and provide a milieu for the characters. What's more, isn't exploring ideas through the medium of place simply more satisfying for the reader?'

Let's leave our friends to their Paris dinner party while we ponder their ideas. Regardless of Beatrice's and Christophe's love of the philosophic abstract, I'm with Fabian. Whilst Kafka and Sartre rank highly on my list of favourite authors, for me the uniqueness and vibrancy that are evoked through a powerful sense of place add a tangible layer of depth and complexity that can lift literature out of the mere recounting of a story, and into a richly sensual experience that transports us, takes us elsewhere, invites us on that journey into the unknown that underpins so much of our cultural story-telling.

My first novel takes its name from India's southern-most town. Kanyakumari is typically south Indian with bustling markets, vibrant temples, a profusion of people, rickshaws, scooters, cows and dogs all contributing to the general clamour and all set against the back drop of the meeting place of three oceans; the Arabian Sea, the Bay of Bengal and the Indian Ocean. Here, the towering statue of the great Tamil philosopher-poet Thiruvalluvar stands sentinel from his little island in the bay, surveying a town quite literally at the end of the earth. Kanyakumari has no airport and the train journey from Delhi, India's capital city, takes around 50 hours. The appeal of taking my readers to such a richly sensuous and enigmatic place was irresistible. This, however, was not the only reason I chose Kanyakumari as my book's setting.

In my opinion all childhood profundity happens at the age of eight, and it was at that age that I first became aware of a dream. It wasn't an actual dream, but rather an image, an idea, a shade. A sense of an archetypal tale began to form in my imagination, a tale that was never to leave me. I don't know where it came from — fairy-tales perhaps, the myths and legends that unbound themselves from the confines of their pages and whispered to my sub-consciousness mind. Or perhaps it was simply an eight-year-olds expression of the mysteries inherent in growing up? I don't know, but from wherever it came, the beauty of what I dreamed defied my ability to fully express it. The story began, as do all self-respecting romances, with a quest.

Quests by their very nature are tough. We know their beginning and we know what we seek but what happens between is a challenge whose purpose is to lead us away from what is familiar and onto the road to transformation. I looked into the heart of my quest and saw a dark path winding off into some undefined future. And I knew that what lay at its end was so profound, so vast in its import, that if I reached it, I would be forever changed. Perhaps the quest was about coming of age, becoming the adult I'd eventually be, finding wholeness, or finding home. I don't know. I called it 'The Search for the Big Orange Poetry Flower.'

And so, I had to look for this flower. I knew that the instant I laid my eyes on its petals, breathed its perfume, that at once all the poetry, all the music, all the creative intoxication of the universe would be released, and my soul, unable to resist, would follow it out of my body and into the vastness that lies beyond time, merging, becoming one with the great unity on which true reality is built. The quest would be over and I would be complete. One more thing I knew, even all those years ago: that my search would end in India.

It was to be many years before I travelled there. I grew my hair long, I found causes to fight for and I wrote some dismal teenage poetry about my quest, but I, perhaps like most, became caught up in the mundane excitement of education, family and career, and my orange flower was left to lie waiting inside the fragility of my memory. But I always knew I'd go to India someday. And finally, one unremarkable springtime, I went.

I hadn't intended *Kanyakumari* to be a novel. On that first trip, I found myself overflowing with emotions, impressions and questions and I began writing in my journal on the flight home as a way to process what I felt. I didn't stop writing and over the coming weeks and months, characters began to emerge, the beginnings of a plot, an intrigue. Like my old quest, I didn't know how the story would end, but I trusted my intuition and I trusted India. And it began to dawn on me that I was writing a book. It was a most happy revelation and I returned to India twice more to immerse myself and my story in the colours, the smells, the sounds, in the pulsating, confounding, enriching world that is India. Here is a little taste:

As Gina wandered slowly and randomly through the borrowed streets she thought about the Tiger sanctuary and wondered if it was worth trying to get there. She thought vaguely about going to the bus station to find out which bus would take her there but knew that the chaos and commotion she would find would make her feel dizzy; better to go later or maybe tomorrow. She kept walking, not at all sure where she was going, allowing herself to be bumped and jostled along by the busy people hurrying around her. How on earth were there so many rushing people in this small town, she thought tetchily, where could they all be going? She tripped, grazing the side of her foot on the uneven road surface, swore to herself inaudibly and stumbled on. A moped carrying three people and a huge bag of something sped past too close to her, hooting and someone shouted. Was he shouting at her? Gina looked around and jumped back quickly as more mopeds zoomed past, some of them carrying impossible loads, one of them carrying something that resembled a fridge. She stumbled into a young Indian man wearing jeans, good shoes and white shirtsleeves, carrying a briefcase and talking loudly in Malayalam into a mobile phone. He raised his arms at his sides in a gesture of frustration as Gina mumbled an embarrassed apology. Someone was laughing and she turned, feeling disorientated and bewildered. There seemed to be people and mopeds rushing everywhere and Gina felt herself sweating and swaying in the rising heat and confusion. She ploughed on, and pushed through a group of ragged, giggling youths who were taunting a skinny dog with a stick, past some leathery, chattery old men wearing faded white Punjabi pyjamas, drinking chai outside a ramshackle café, two fat women in saris and lots of gold jewellery debating loudly and animatedly about something in a shop doorway. A bewildered looking old man wearing a dirty ragged kurta who appeared to have only one arm lurched towards her saying something in a garbled voice. He stared into her face, his eyes rheumy, his open mouth revealing an incomplete set of uneven black teeth. Gina looked around, her eyes wide with alarm, but the man shuffled past her, mumbling to himself. Faces began to merge, a cacophony of chattering, shouting, laughter, of people, dogs, mopeds.

I see all journeys as quests. Even if we're not 'searching' in the spiritual sense, I believe that when we travel, we are looking to inhabit the world in a new way, to experience ourselves differently. I think too that this is often why we read. No-one ends where they begin, neither in life nor in fiction. My 'Indian quest', my search for this Big Orange Poetry Flower wasn't for me the classic search for a 'true self'. Maybe, over time it had become an expression of that bitter-sweet yearning for home that the Welsh call '*hiraeth*' that we all sometimes feel, even when we are at the place we call home. I saw in India that, regardless of colour, creed or country, what unites us is stronger and more vital than what separates us. Even so, India to me remains a very foreign place. I connected with it strongly but trying to understand a culture and a way of life so very different to our own is akin to learning a new language. Only gradually do we begin to grasp its enigmas.

For me, evoking a powerful sense of India by creating a novel from the meandering stream of consciousness that appeared on the pages of my journal allowed me explore what it is to be an 'outsider.' Not understanding the customs, the culture or the languages, my characters struggle to understand their surroundings and the people around them. The foreignness of the country reflects their growing sense of isolation and their need to resolve this. Perhaps this was the meaning of my quest? Creating a sense of place that is vivid and vibrant in its depiction of India enabled me to explore this sense of 'differentness', of 'otherness' we all sometimes feel, even when we're not in a foreign country. India then was not only a wonderfully evocative backdrop to my novel but was, in a sense, a metaphor for that existential loneliness we feel when we don't understand our relationship with the world around us.

So, did I find my Big Orange Poetry Flower? Well, over the years I've spent a lot of time in India, travelling, working, learning and what I've discovered is a country I don't understand, where I feel alien yet at home, infuriated and fascinated, a country that is so hard to be in but so difficult to leave, whose people, religions, cities and landscapes have captured my imagination so deeply that the only way to process it is artistically. The Big Orange Poetry Flower turned out to be my novel and I realised that in *Kanyakumari*.

And so to Paris. Which, by way of those strange synchronicities we often call coincidence is for me connected with India, because it was there that I met my French partner. The rest, as they say is history, and I now live with him in the City of Light.

Being a British expat in France is a life full of small and sometimes not so small discoveries. Although not as extreme as in India, I'm fascinated by the cultural differences that exist between the British and the French. There is often the assumption that because our two countries are geographically and historically close, that French and British cultures are, if not identical, at least mutually understandable. And to a certain extent this is of course true. We are both Christian based but multi-faith countries and we share a similar time-line in terms of economic, industrial and technological development. There are differences though, and those differences are more than just the food (calf's pancreas? Seriously?) and the obvious fact that we speak different languages. When is it wrong to use *'vous'* rather than the informal *'tu'* for example? (I imagined that because my French is based solely on using the *'vous'* form, this could never offend anyone. I was mistaken.) The fact that the French serve cheese before dessert was a revelation to me and I experienced some decidedly perplexed looks when I first entertained Parisian friends. And French colloquialisms — what *does* it mean to *'put a rabbit'* or to *'have the cockroach'*? As was the case in India, I find myself to be an outsider, living in a country that I love but where I don't fully fit.

Paris — its name alone conjures a place of romance, of sophistication, a city of artistic and architectural beauty where idealists and philosophers come together in salons and bars to debate passionately, where for men and women alike, chic is nothing short of a religion, and where moody writers may be seen scribbling intensely in corners of dark cafés, chain-smoking Gauloises and drinking cheap wine. Apart from the cigarettes, I myself have done my best to adopt and uphold this noble tradition! But of course, for most Parisians, their home town is simply the backdrop to their everyday lives, where cafés and wine and *la vie créatif* have their place, but so too do traffic and shopping and battling the rush-hour metro. In my second novel, *The Geranium Woman* I enjoy setting the ordinary life of a Parisian business-woman against the backdrop of this most captivating of cities.

At the start of this chapter we left our dinner party-goers exploring the importance of a sense of place. If a sense of place is important, it follows that the next question is how to go about creating and conveying that sense, and I thought a lot about this when planning my second novel. It was an interesting challenge to draw out not what was alienating and different as I had done in *Kanyakumari*, but to find what was customary and make that fascinating. One of the things I asked myself was when we think about a place that is meaningful to us what exactly is it that we recall? Certainly, what happened, the people we were with, the emotions we felt give the place its significance and ensure that it takes its place in our memory. And central to creating meaning and memory, is the power of our sensory experiences — what we see, hear, smell, feel and taste often remain with us long after we've forgotten other details.

For me, invoking a sense of place involves creating an interplay between the scene and all five of the characters' senses. As is true in life, whatever the characters are doing or saying, they will undoubtedly be affected by how the setting is impacting on their senses and this will contribute to how they feel, how they act and what they say. In addition, for the reader sensory information creates a backdrop to the plot in the same way that a stage setting sets the scene in a play; ever-present, contextualising, providing a *mise-en-scène* for the narrative.

Let's take our sense of sight — a primary filter of all that makes up our world. What we see is at the forefront of our sensory experience, contributing powerfully to what creates the uniqueness of a place. Writers tend to routinely describe what people and places look like, and when done well can take us quickly to that feeling of being 'inside' a story. I find though that focusing away from the obvious and picking out lesser noticed details can help avoid clichés and stereotypes and can zoom in on what makes the setting unique. These are the kinds of details that create a more intimate sense of place. A bee buzzing in a window, used metro tickets on a station floor, moss growing on a building — it is this kind of askance view that can mean the difference between the reader knowing where the scene is set, and feeling themselves at the place itself. In the following extract from *The Geranium Woman*, two women are sitting in a Paris café:

> The café was almost full and a line of men in business suits was standing at the bar. I noticed that the floor was littered with sugar wrappers and as though I'd conjured him up, a waiter with a broom appeared and started to sweep them away. I looked at Marine and smiled. Once again, she smiled back. I felt relieved when the waitress arrived with our drinks and a little dish of olives. I picked up my glass. 'Cheers,' I said. We clinked our glasses together and each took a sip. I ate an olive. Neither of us said anything until we both started to speak at the same time.

For me, it's important to use not only the visual sense but the other four senses as well. We know how important smell is in our memories. Often, a particular fragrance can trigger a long-forgotten person or place. I can't smell the aroma of a lovely cup of tea without picturing my Grand-mother sitting in her armchair, a floral patterned bone-china cup and saucer balanced on her knee as she reads out the questions of our Saturday afternoon quiz. And the power of smell is well known in the selling-industry, with estate agents suggesting that we have coffee brewing when showing prospective buyers around a house and supermarkets pumping the smell of baking bread into their stores. Smell stimulates feeling, whether it be well-being, or revulsion. Whatever my characters are doing, they can't shut off their sense of smell and this creates opportunities for the writer. Weaving the smell of incense, of exhaust smoke, cut-grass, cheap perfume, sweat, wet-dog into the narrative or the dialogue can take the reader directly and intimately to the setting and provide information that doesn't rely on 'telling' (the writer's worst enemy) but that serves to show the reader the background and context of a scene. In the next extract from *The Geranium Woman*, our main character has returned to her father's Paris apartment for the first time since his funeral:

The first thing I noticed was the smell. Pipe tobacco and coffee. I closed my eyes. The scent was so quintessentially him, that I almost believed it could be possible to slip like a thief between the folds of its substance, to a time that hadn't after all disappeared, but had simply glazed over, like at a meeting, where you momentarily close your eyes and on re-opening them find that the same pink man is still talking about the same profit margin. It was as though, if I opened my eyes now, I could steal back the time that separated me from him and, pushing open the salon door, I would find my father sitting in his usual chair amid a swirl of tobacco smoke, pipe in hand, an *allongé* cooling on the end table whilst his glasses slipped down his nose as he read the headlines in *Libération*.

The sense of sound can achieve a similar effect. Sounds are more than just noise, and drawing the readers' attention to them can create not only atmosphere but can also serve to anchor the ambiance to a specific place and time. I was fascinated to read recently about a 'museum of lost sounds' which captured for posterity noises that we no longer hear — the clacking of typewriter keys for example, the crackle of a vinyl record, or the sound of a 1980's telephone, when the dial was released. When I imagine this sound, I am instantly transported to my childhood home, where I would sneak up to the hall-table, glancing furtively around to make sure my parents weren't about, before grabbing the receiver of our recently purchased onyx telephone, that most forbidden piece of magic, dial my best friend's number, cursing the fact that my fear of getting caught had no impact on its speed, and, cupped hand around the mouth-piece, hurriedly make whispered plans for our next escapade. All that memory contained within one simple sound. It offers powerful possibilities for the novelist.

Touch and taste — such sensual experiences — even words like lips, tongue, skin, finger-tips, spice, pungent convey so much. But these senses are sometimes overlooked in fiction writing, perhaps because they are so specific. Both though, can be potent triggers for our emotions and again, I like to link them to a landscape or a place, giving the reader visceral signs rather than authorial intrusion. The feel of sun on burning skin, of warm rain on an upturned face, dry grass scratching the soles of bare feet — all are more evocative than blandly stating that the place was hot. Similarly, and especially when the setting is a foreign one, taste, even (and perhaps especially) when not the point of a scene can convey so much that adds to its richness.

I love the challenge of creating a narrative which flows between the internal and the external. It feels more natural, perhaps because this is the way we experience our lives. We are at once aware of our thoughts and our emotions as well as what is happening around us. Writing which doesn't acknowledge this flow can feel flat, lacking the finesse of a more integrated piece. Sitting here in my study, for example, I am focused very firmly on what I'm writing, whether it's thought-provoking and interesting enough, how to make it more so. But I'm also aware of the rows of books on their shelves in my peripheral vision, of the fact that the room feels a little cold, that the coffee I made earlier still smells good, the rain against the balcony doors and the loud French of some men in the street below. The internal and the external co-exist and intermingle, making my experience here at my desk complex and multi-layered.

I'm a great believer in the power of mirrors. Mirrors do a kind of magic — they reflect back to us that which we can't see alone. Here in Paris I host a salon called Paris Writers' Working Lunches where each week, a small group of writers meet at my apartment, enjoy lunch together and spend the afternoon acting as mirrors, giving honest critiques of one another's work. I find my colleagues' feedback invaluable and I'd recommend that fledging writers keen to hone their work find or start such a group. One of the things we often notice with new writers is a tendency to 'set the scene' at the start of a story or chapter by beginning with a paragraph or so of descriptive detail. This can sometimes leave the rest of the chapter feeling one-dimensional and members of our group often suggest that rather than giving it in one expository lump, a far more subtle approach is to weave such detail through the entire narrative, including dialogue. This can be a powerful tool for the developing writer, a way to enhance realism, drawing the reader's attention to the setting without being 'told', and of layering sensory and other detail into the fabric of the story in a natural way, building complexity, context, meaning and background. In this way, the writer is not simply describing where the scene is taking place, but is taking the reader there, intimately, sensually, unequivocally.

Perhaps this is a good time to return to the party and see what our friends have made of the subject.

'*Zut alors!*' Natalie nearly wobbled off Christophe's knees on which she was somewhat precariously perched. Her voice competed with Joe Dassin who had supplanted Jacques Brel and was reminding us lyrically that '*…this isn't going to change the world.*' We ignored him.

'*Bien sûr…*' Natalie cried! 'Of course 'place' is fundamental. It is a natural, philosophical 'fact', *n'est-ce pas? Certainement*, most of our experiences can't be detached from it.'

Christophe reached across the clutter associated with the cheeseboard, which had been shoved aside to make way for a bottle of Sauterne and a bowl of raspberries. Ignoring the spoon, he picked out a fruit, dipped it first into a bowl of *fromage blanc*, then into some brown sugar.

'*C'est délicieux!*' he said, popping the raspberry into Natalie's open mouth and licking sugar from her lips. '*Mais oui Natalie, je suis d'accord, vous avez raison.*'

I smiled at Christophe's about-turn, wondering whether it had anything to do with Natalie's breasts which he was surreptitiously fondling as they nudged against his arm. I squeezed my knees against the foot creeping up my leg.

'*D'accord,*' Christophe repeated, 'Place is the bedrock of our experience. Even our dreams take place *somewhere. Oui*, place holds for us a vital sense of meaning! The novelist would do well to remember this.' He and Natalie clinked glasses and downed what remained in them.

'Indeed,' said Fabian, reaching for the Sauterne. 'A sense of place has strong sense-associations which can transport the reader.' He tipped what remained of the bottle into my glass, winking at me as the last drop plinked in. 'Let's bring the matter out of the abstract,' he said. 'If we think of any major event, whether personal or public, we can usually remember exactly where we were — place acts as a memory anchor for our significant moments.' He paused, shook his head and spoke more quietly. 'Take the *Charlie Hebdo* attack for example. I'd just finished teaching a philosophy class. I was standing by my desk wondering whether I had time for a quick coffee when my colleague rushed in. I remember clearly the sun streaming through the window and highlighting the dust-motes above his head as I tried to make sense of what he was telling me. I imagine all of you remember where you were too.'

'I was in bed,' Natalie said with a wave of her cigarette. 'I'll say no more…'

'I was in *Rue Saint Jacques*, on my way to meet Christophe,' I said, 'when I heard a commotion in a café. I remember peering past the terrace through the open door, the smell of coffee and cigarettes, the red striped shirt of a man who was staring at the television on the wall crying *'oh mon dieu, oh mon dieu…!'*

Christophe closed his eyes and nodded and we were silent for a long moment. I noticed with surprise that the rain had stopped. I watched the candle-lit faces of Natalie, Fabian and Christophe through the cigarette haze, and smiled as Joe Dassin sang a toast to our unspoken *esprit de corps*: *'To life, to love, to our nights, to our days, to the endless return of fortune …'*

'Well, it seems that we are of one mind,' Fabian said at last. 'We're all agreed that there is a power in *place* — in all its grandness and its minutiae, in its foreignness and familiarity, a power that goes beyond a merely cerebral recounting of a tale, to a sensuality, an intimacy, where, for the length of a book, we step out of our world and so fully into a new one that we forget ourselves. And after all, isn't that what a good story is about?'

Places
John Barnie

In Abergavenny, at the bottom of Priory Road, the River Gavenny runs between steep sandstone banks overgrown with bushes and trees. When I knew it as a child, there was a narrow strip of meadow bordered by a thick hedge that closed off access to the stream. It was 'private', but we knew where you could crawl through a gap, and the bushes and tangled patches of brambles above the stream became our playground.

Opposite the entrance to Priory Road the banks were at their steepest and in the middle of the stream was a large rock which the water dashed against with such force you had to shout to be heard as the river swirled round into a deep pool. One day Geoff Downs, the leader of our gang, stripped off and jumped in, a skinny figure clutching his arms to his body and shivering. The rest of us leaned over the bank, holding on to saplings, to see what he would do. The water came up to his chest and Geoff made breaststroke movements with his hands, then bent so his right cheek was almost touching the surface of the stream, looking up at us intently.

— I nearly had it, he shouted, claiming when he hauled himself up onto the grass that he had tickled a big trout but it had got away just when he was about to throw it up on the bank.

I never saw any fish in the Gavenny, then or later, but Geoff was two years older than us and because we wanted to believe it, we did — imagination being more powerful than truth when you are ten or eleven.

On the opposite bank the land rose steeply to a high sandstone wall surrounding Pen-y-val Lunatic Asylum. On a winter evening I could see its barred windows from our house bright with lights and sometimes a head and shoulders in silhouette as a figure moved across my line of vision. The buildings were tall, built in the nineteenth century, looking very much like a prison. They were over-topped by a line of ancient horse chestnuts whose canopies contained a large rookery. At sunset, summer and winter, the rooks congregated and flew out in a great flock across the Gavenny and over our house, cawing and flapping, then wheeling back to settle for the night in the trees. You could never quite forget the Asylum if you lived on Priory Road, it was there, sombre, with its tall barred windows, a refusal, a great No.

During the Second World War a family had been billeted in our house while my father was in the Army, but when the War ended they moved to Ross House at the bottom of Priory Road. I went there often, as to me by then they were an unofficial 'aunt' and 'uncle'. Their front garden was raised fourteen feet or more above the street as it shelved steeply toward the river. From that vantage point I could look across the meadow and the Gavenny into an exercise yard on the other side of the Asylum wall. There, on the right, was a structure with a conical roof, divided into sections with wooden seats like a Victorian seaside shelter. Patients sat in it listlessly while others wandered up and down, back and fore. One woman had long grey hair down to her waist, she talked loudly and angrily to herself. Some screamed; some shouted. In my memory of them, they were all dressed in grey. This was in the late 1940s and 1950s, before the development of psychotropic drugs which revolutionised mental health care. In Pen-y-val, I somehow knew, there were locked wards and padded cells and people in strait-jackets. Sometimes a patient escaped, and there would be the long-drawn-out wail of a siren and a man in black uniform and peaked cap came knocking on doors along Priory Road, warning housewives to be on their guard. Whoever they were and wherever they went, I never saw any of the escapees.

Much later, in 1965, my younger brother had a schizophrenic breakdown. He wasn't taken to Pen-y-val but to Maindiff Court, a modern psychiatric unit a mile and a half up the road, where he was treated with ECT and drugs, blunt instruments which most of the time contained his illness but never cured him. That was when the barred windows of Pen-y-val came down on our family.

Rivers and streams were important to me as a child. When I was in grammar school, I graduated from the Gavenny to the Usk and once knew every yard of a two-mile stretch from Abergavenny upstream to Llanwenarth. I knew where sand martins nested in the rust-red banks and where you could see kingfishers and dippers; and where bullheads and loach could be netted in the cold glittering shallows; and sticklebacks in warm backwaters; and shoals of dace, fleeing in flood pools like a quiver of brown arrows from my shadow.

There was one place where I always paused, at the monument to the boy who drowned. This was an obelisk made of concrete, about four feet high, enclosed in a square of ornamental railings. Perhaps my parents told me it was a monument, because there was nothing on the obelisk to explain why it was there, and I never found out its date, though it must have been from the early twentieth century.

When I knew it first, the memorial stood in a field, five or six yards from the river and the deep water where the boy had drowned, but the Usk slowly alters course over the alluvial plain, undermining banks that collapse in flood water brought down from the mountains after heavy rain. Over the years the river moved toward the monument until one side of the railings perched on the bank, then hung over the edge. At last it disappeared. Then it was the turn of the obelisk, the foundations exposed above the turbid flow. One day it too was gone, lying on its side in the mud. After a while the rest of the railings went, and it was as if the monument had never been. By now I suppose the railings have rotted away, but the obelisk may still be there buried on the river bed, or rolled in winter on a slow, heavy journey to the sea.

When I was a boy, I was obliged to attend Sunday morning service at St Mary's Church in Monk Street until I was confirmed in 1956. Then I stopped. The light was always grey in the Protestant nave, the only colour coming from a spray of flowers arranged by the women, and stained glass in the altar window. One Sunday, I became aware of a pattering sound. The hymns and organ drowned it out, but when the echo to the 'Amen' faded, it was there. Eventually I traced it to a small bird, a house sparrow, that had somehow become trapped in the church and fluttered up and down the window, attracted to the light. It cheeped as it pressed itself against the brightly coloured glass only to sink exhausted to the sill. Eventually the service ended and we filed out into sunshine, leaving the sparrow to its prison. I never found out what happened to it.

These are just three scenes from the patchwork of memory, one lasting a brief hour, the others spread over a number of years ending when I left Abergavenny at the age of nineteen.

It was the beginning of twenty years spent living in cities — Birmingham, Nottingham, Copenhagen — but the city never caught my imagination and I have only written one book about the time I was lost in the anonymous crowds of its streets, a dystopian collage of prose poems and prose (*The City*, Gomer, 1993).

What has meaning for me is the landscape in which I grew up, the world of the Usk valley with its rivers and streams, its hills and woods, its farms, small towns and villages. It is a landscape which is real and symbolic, imprinted on my mind from an early an age. The patients in the exercise yard at Pen-y-val, the 'trout tickling' in the Gavenny, the sparrow trapped in St Mary's, the destruction of the monument, all appear in barely disguised form in an autobiographical novella, *The Confirmation* (Gomer, 1992), where symbolic value is an undertow to the surface realism.

It is many years since I lived in Abergavenny, and I could not write that piece now. When you are born into a landscape, it inhabits you, so you cannot disentangle it from what you are. When you leave, however, there is a parting of the ways which at first you do not recognise. Time passes and in doing so it changes you, and changes the towns and villages, the streams and hills you knew so well; you travel in different directions and the landscape dwindles as if viewed from a departing train.

The danger of continuing to dwell in such a landscape is that the writer slides by degrees into nostalgia, describing what once was but is no more in a way which becomes artistically suspect. Today, many years after I left the Usk valley, my experience there only surfaces in poetry in the form of images and symbols refined of their specific location. So a short poem I wrote recently has the long-disappeared obelisk as its focus:

The Monument
(to a boy who drowned)

The river is a snake
that swallows all it can;
it took the boy, the obelisk,
the railings, the man
he never became
and the grief of the parents;
it takes the meadows
and rolls them in winter floods
down to the sea.

I had no intention of omitting the location of the obelisk on the bank of the Usk; in fact when I sat down to write, I had no intention at all. The poem simply came; the years of watching the bank erode and the monument disappear, distilled into a symbol of the frailty of human love and grief; the vanity of the monuments we erect before a nature that is greater than ourselves, destroying and creating with perfect indifference.

When I came upon the monument as a child, the obelisk was already old, the railings long unpainted and rusting. I thought often of the dead boy and never knew who he was. I thought of the parents, too, who were doubtless also dead by the time I walked the riverbank to Llanwenarth, their heartache over.

The image of the river as a snake is another distillation, of standing many a time on the brow of the Deri, looking down on the town and the valley where the Usk wound through meadows, silver-grey, into distant haze toward Newport and the sea.

The sparrow trapped in St Mary's has also emerged in this way. *Footfalls in the Silence* (Cinnamon, 2014), is a memoir covering the period up to my departure for Copenhagen in 1969. As such, it tries to recall the past with a degree of realism, but in a passage reflecting on my drinking habits, the bird suddenly appeared, unannounced, as I wrote:

> I wonder how many barrels, especially of wine, I have drunk in a lifetime — how they would look stacked in a dimly-lit warehouse where a sparrow cheeps among rafters unable to find its way out through the broken pane.

Here the sparrow is divorced from the context in which I experienced it in Abergavenny. In *The Confirmation* the incident might be assigned a symbolic value by some readers — an image for the 'soul' or 'spirit' perhaps. But as an atheist for whom there is no reality beyond the material universe these concepts have no meaning and were not part of my intention. In *Footfalls in the Silence* where the memory has been reassigned to an imaginary context, the symbolic value is clearer — a sense, which most of us have at times, that we are trapped in a life we never asked for. Beyond the tall windows of church or warehouse there is light and life but on the other side of the glass. Perhaps there is a broken pane through which you can escape to re-engage with the world but, for now, you cannot find it.

Interpreting one's own work is dangerous, however, because the writer runs the risk of becoming overly self-conscious about processes that are best left to themselves. It is a particular temptation for poets doing readings where there is a fine line between introducing a poem in a way that prepares the audience for its reception and explaining it away before it has been read. There is nothing worse than a reading in which the introduction is so long the poem becomes an afterthought. Self-explication must also be a pitfall for writers who earn a living teaching 'creative writing'.

*

For thirty years now, I have lived in Comins Coch, a village a mile and a half outside Aberystwyth; it is the longest I have lived in one place. The area has a hugely varied landscape, ranging from farmland and woods to the upland moors of the Cambrian Mountains, from the salt marsh of Cors Fochno to the dunes of Ynys-las, the miles of sand from the Dyfi estuary to Borth, and the sea cliffs along the coast to Aberystwyth. It is only in the past few years, however, that I have internalised this landscape in a way that makes it available to me as a writer.

In 2009, I had the idea I would like to write a book of poems about wildflowers. All I knew was the poems would be short and would have close-up photographs of each flower on a facing page. I decided, too, that I would only write about flowers I could find within walking distance of Comins Coch, an area of approximately eight square miles. I have known the commonest wildflowers all my life and started writing poems about them almost immediately, but it is birds I know best, and the project set me off on a learning curve. I obtained a digital camera and spent the spring and summer of 2010 wandering about the countryside, photographing all the flowers I could find in hedgerows, woods, along the cliffs, in the dunes, and on the foreshore. It could be embarrassing caught kneeling in a lane to get a close-up of common toadflax; or on my hands and knees in the dunes, photographing marsh orchids at ground level — 'You look like a man on a mission', a holidaymaker said, as he passed on the way to the beach.

By early autumn I had photographed some two hundred species and had identified most with the aid of Marjorie Blamey and Christopher Grey-Wilson's *Wild Flowers of Britain and Northern Europe* and C.A.M.

107

Lindman's *Billeder af Nordens Flora*. Those months involved looking at this landscape in detail — the way clumps of thrift hung quivering in updraft at a cliff edge; hound's-tongue with grey, furred leaves and small flowers the colour of dried blood thriving in the arid dunes; and slender St. John's wort, inconspicuous in hedge-bank grass and easily overlooked, yet with the most delicate yellow petals when you bent to see.

And I discovered an old truth, that naming is part of seeing. Flowers I would have walked passed and merely noted as 'yellow' or 'blue' now became bird's-foot trefoil and sheep's-bit with an identity I could relate to — just as humans are an undifferentiated mass in the streets until your eyes pluck out one whose name you know.

The book that resulted, *A Year of Flowers* (Gomer), appeared in 2011. It made me realise that after many years of living here, Ceredigion had become my landscape, and that the Usk valley I had known so well was now a geological stratum of the mind, only outcrops revealing the formation of what was once a living world.

Landscape for me has always been layered. Growing up in Abergavenny it was impossible to be unaware of our human past as a palimpsest on the land, something I tried to express in one section of *Footfalls in the Silence*:

I have always been attracted to ruins. There were the castles for a start, especially Skenfrith, Grosmont and White Castles, strung along the border and within easy reach of Abergavenny by bicycle. I liked their red sandstone, eroded to grey by wind and rain, the battlements and towers — especially White Castle's, looking out on undulating fields and hedgerows and beyond to the faded blue of the Black Mountains. I knew little of their history even after I began research into the Middle Ages as a postgraduate. I was drawn to their atmosphere, a certain resonance with which I felt at home.

It was the ruined farms of the Black Mountains that I found most appealing. Walking up a steep rutted lane I would come upon an isolated building, a sheepfold perhaps, or a barn, its roof of stone fallen in, the wood of its rafters rotten and gone. A wall might have collapsed, a jumble of stones with thick coats of moss. Always there would be nettles, and sometimes a sheep or two startled into flight at my appearance. The wind tugged at these walls as it did the walls of the castles. It was a lonely world, as if those who had prised the stones from shallow quarries in the hillsides and raised the walls, had one day got up and gone, leaving nothing of themselves except the labour of their hands.

These ruins became identified in my mind with Wordsworth's poem 'Michael', and 'the straggling heap of unhewn stones', meant for a sheepfold the old man lacked the heart to build.

In 1981 I visited Lybster in Caithness where my paternal grandfather had grown up before making the long journey to the South Wales coalfield as a lad in the 1880s. His family had been crofters and after some enquiry, together with my cousins Geoff and Alan and my wife Helle, we found the croft where he had been born. It was a low stone building with the byre at one end and the living quarters at the other. Although abandoned as a dwelling years before, it must have been used for storage until quite recently; part of the roof was still thatched with clumps of turf where the rafters had not collapsed.

This is how it would have started when farms in the Black Mountains were let go during the agricultural crises of the nineteenth century, a roof stone slipping, a window frame rotting, a tinkle of breaking glass that nobody heard.

In Ceredigion it is geology's deep time that attracts as I walk cliffs whose strata were laid down between 400 and 500 million years ago — a time scale so vast it cannot be conceptualised in human terms. The strata have been bent and folded, sometimes into the vertical, by the immense pressure of crustal movements, and now are being eroded by weather and the battering of the waves. Each spring, when I start walking the cliffs from Clarach to Borth, there is some point where the coastal path has been rerouted because of a cliff fall; or there is an ominous fissure, a slice of the cliff detached and lowered as if after an earthquake, ready to collapse plunging into the Bay.

And there on the surface is life — wheatears fluttering from fence post to fence post as I advance; the scolding *wheet-chak-chak* of stonechats; at my feet in the jumble of grasses and bracken, thrift, sea campion, harebell, sheep's-bit; the tiny blue butterflies whose species I have never been able to identify for sure, and daytime moths like the six-spot burnet. When we see gnats dancing in a shaft of sunlight it is hard not to be aware of their fleeting existence — how long do they live, a few days? Walking the cliffs, however, the world is so vibrant you have the feeling this could never end. Then you look down at layer upon layer of 400-million-year-old rock. Sunlight had shone there too summer on summer, but on life forms very different to the ones we are familiar with. Now they are gone, lost in cold stone where occasionally, if you are lucky, you might find the fossil remains of a bivalve. On my shelves I have fossils of a trilobite, crinoids mown down, their stalks beginning to disarticulate, a small fish three inches long, the larva of a dragonfly, life that once was crawling, swimming, waving in the currents, though they are not from around here where, for most part, the rocks are empty and silent.

Nowhere is this process more evident than at Borth where in the shifting sands the remains of a drowned forest appear at low tide which provided the title for my collection *The Forest Under the Sea* (Cinnamon, 2010). During the last Ice Age, the land extended eleven kilometres out into what is now Cardigan Bay. As the climate ameliorated, this became a dense forest, mostly of pine, birch and oak; but the melting of the ice inundated the forest turning it into a marsh about 4000 years ago; then another forest sprang up, only to be inundated in its turn 2000 years later. It is the remains of these trees that can be seen at Borth at low tide. Usually there are only stumps, the wood soft and easily marked by a fingernail, but sometimes there are many trunks lying in the same orientation as if blown down by a gale. The forest was exposed in a spectacular way after the winter storms of 2014, including large slabs of semi-fossilised peat, the remains of the marsh in which the trees had died.

This is the point of exchange between deep time and the surface where we live. The exposed remains of the forest no doubt gave rise to the medieval legend of Cantre'r Gwaelod, the drowned kingdom under the waters of the Bay. I have a fragment of bark from a pine tree, picked up on the shore, darkened to a dusky brown by minerals in the bog where it lay for many centuries. It sits on a windowsill with spiny cockleshells, a bivalve with a tiny round hole bored in the shell by a marauding whelk, a razor shell, a cluster of oyster shells soldered together hugger-mugger, all collected on the sands between Borth and the Dyfi estuary.

It is this interplay between the present and deep time which fascinates and which found expression in a number of poems in *The Forest Under the Sea*. Borth itself, or at least lower Borth, sheltered behind a bank of pebbles and surrounded on three sides by sea-level fields and the salt marsh of Cors Fochno, is fact and symbol of the precarious nature of the surface world where we live:

Borth

From the perspective of the
inhabitants, Borth has
always been there with the sea's

breathing the other side of the wall,
and balsa wood fleets of gulls
at high tide; at low

the drowned forest of the
Cantref, oak and pine, steps out
of the sand

with a different assemblage of facts
that don't add up to the
long street and the bus

dwindling in parallel
lines to Ynys Las where,
for now, the story ends.

That sense of transience is all around if you walk the sands from the Dyfi estuary to Borth. Above is the wide sky, to the north the faded mountains of

Gwynedd, and always the sea, laying its waves tirelessly on the shore. It is easy to become absorbed in the grandeur, but look down at your feet and there on the tide line is the detritus of the world — the shells of cockles and other bivalves, tiny pink crabs, acorns and beech mast brought down by rivers, stranded jellyfish, a dogfish, goose barnacles, a sodden herring gull, all likely to disappear without leaving a trace that they ever existed:

Razor Shells at Ynys Las

Hundreds of barbers here
for a convention except
they've abandoned their blades, as if
they remembered the moon's eye

sliced through in that
film and couldn't go
on, leaving the sand to be
clean shaved by the tide.

The mind too has its Cantre'r Gwaelod, where those you once knew surface like the remains of the drowned forest, only to be buried again:

Cantre'r Gwaelod

I'm trying to recall the wreckage of my parents' lives,
my brother's,

confounded with claws and tree stumps on the shore
as

memory sweeps their images
out and in.

There are two kinds of imaginative writing about place, one of which is travel writing. The author selects a place, reads up on it perhaps, then travels there, meeting people, observing, taking notes. He or she may live in the chosen area for a several months, or it may be a fleeting visit. The travel writer has to be receptive to atmosphere, have an eye for detail, an ability to take things in at speed, and recreate what is seen in a way which convinces the reader of its authenticity. This is 'outsider writing'; the author is not a part of what is observed, or is only so in an ambiguous way. If the writer is honest, there is an inevitable sense of distance; an awareness of the fact that eventually he or she will move on.

Place in poetry and in certain kinds of fiction is different. It is internalised by the poet or novelist, becoming part of the core of the writer's being, both real and symbolic at the same time. This is true of Wordsworth's Westmoreland, Robinson Jeffers' Carmel and Big Sur, Les Murray's Bunyah, and R.S. Thomas's Manafon; in fiction William Faulkner's Mississippi and Randolph Stow's Western Australia are examples.

The difference between this kind of writing about place and travel writing is that you do not choose the place, the place chooses you, and there is nothing to be done about it. We have all been to places that have fascinated us, and it is tempting as a poet to try to write out of the experience. Sometimes this works, but mostly what is produced is travel writing in verse and is not among the poet's best work. Jeffers' Big Sur and R.S. Thomas's Manafon are mythic places where significant things happen. At one level, both Jeffers and Thomas were outsiders, of course, since they did not grow up in the places they wrote about; but they grew *into* them, finding deep correspondences between themselves and the wild country of mid California or the bare hills of mid Wales. Place for them sparked an imaginative leap which drove the poetry.

R.S. Thomas, it might be argued, remained an outsider at Manafon more so than Jeffers at Carmel, debarred by his role as priest in the Church in Wales, by class and education, from ever becoming fully absorbed into the mindset of that world. This is true, and the Iago Prytherch poems about the hard life of the hill farmer during and after the Second World War stress this alienation; but Prytherch is also an objective correlative for the harsh conditions of the poet's inner world — recognition of like with like being part of the imaginative equation.

When I was in New York a few years ago with Twm Morys, Iwan Llwyd and Iwan Bala, they were much taken with the legend of Gwales and the warriors who feasted there for eighty years with Brân's severed head, until one of them opened the forbidden Cornwall-facing door and the spell was broken. That was another kind of place. Gwales is said to be Grassholm off the Pembrokeshire coast, but that is not what interested them; what counted was the mythic place, the paradise that was lost.

Gwales did not resonate for me, as it did for them, and I doubt I could ever write about it; but Cantre'r Gwaelod, the legendary kingdom sunk beneath Cardigan Bay does. Like Gwales, you can never go there, but you can see its remains in the trunks and stumps of the drowned forest at Borth; because Cantre'r Gwaelod is both legend and fact, based on the great upheavals that occurred in Northern Europe ten thousand years ago as the last Ice Age ended and sea levels rose relentlessly.

I think about this every time I walk among the semi-fossilised tree stumps, or look down from the cliffs at

Sarn Cynfelyn — the remains of a medial moraine at Wallog, between Clarach and Borth. Sea anglers tell me it is a good place to fish if you know where it lies, stretching many kilometres under the water.

It is perhaps a memory of those conversations in New York and of my inability to respond to the myth of Gwales which so excited the imaginations of Twm and the two Iwans, which prompted a poem in *The Roaring Boys* (Cinnamon, 2012):

Where Would You Prefer to Be?

I wouldn't live in Gwales,
all that shot-putting at the Sun
and shouting the stars out of their sockets,

that head
talking its head off

and the forbidden door,
power's doggy game;
I'd rather stand on the shores of Cantre'r Gwaelod,
watching the Bay turn blue then green then grey,

the sun sweeping in cathedral shafts across the water,
over the sand and the dunes, across Cors Fochno to
the hills,
as gannets dive for fish and cormorants dry their
wings.

I feel easy writing out of Ceredigion now, though it took almost half a lifetime to reach this point. When I first moved to Comins Coch, I headed by instinct for the Cambrian Mountains when I went out for a walk, trying, I suppose, to reproduce the lost world of the Black Mountains and what they had meant to me for so many years. Without a car, though, they were not really accessible, so I started walking the lanes instead, around

Capel Dewi, Capel Madog, Banc-y-Darren and Cefn Llwyd, with far off glimpses of the sea.

It was a long time before it occurred to me to walk the cliffs or the sands at Ynys-las; for though our family went for daytrips to the seaside every summer — to Barry Island, Porthcawl, or Southerndown — it was the foothills of the Black Mountains that I associated myself with. I was not a coastal person; the sea had no resonance for me.

Perhaps it was accident, perhaps it was the need to explore something new, that led me eventually to the coast. Now it is where I prefer to be, absorbed in the ever changing world of water and sky, insects, flowers and birds, yachts and working boats, that each walk spreads before me, as in this poem, also from *The Roaring Boys*:

The View from All-Wen

Seen from the cliff top, crabbers putter flat
against the sea, hooking buoys on deck
and cages; choughs swing out from crevices
with clattering cries just because they can;

there's nothing airy about humans who
do everything to a plan, even the yachters
labouring out of Aberystwyth harbour
planning fun; I suppose the crabs don't know

they're done for in their creepy iron-age
cladding, khaki secateurs snipping at the
light; the choughs have disappeared below my
feet like magicians' apprentices

and water slops against the rocks from
Strumble Head to the blue island mountains of
Pen Llŷn; there's nowhere else to go, north,
south, west, or east, this being home.

Neither Here Nor There —
A Dialogue of Places
Ian Gregson

My sense of place has its origins in the contrast between my upbringing in Manchester and my experience of living, since 1977, in North Wales. The two are not far apart geographically, but they are distant culturally, and that is very much emphasised by the presence of the Welsh language, whose interactions with the Welsh landscape are urgent and vivid. The contrast has therefore impressed upon me a powerful sense that physical place, topography, geology etc, is only one of the components that define what a place means. The corollary of that sense is a conviction, which is constitutive for my work, that place is coloured by cultural point of view, and is therefore deeply unstable and is always in process and is endlessly being altered by shifting subjectivities. So in practice in my writing, place is always filtered through character, which is occasionally a version of my own, but is most often someone made up; this is obvious and natural in fiction, but dramatic monologue is the most frequently used genre in my poems, so there, too, landscape is never presented objectively.

In *Not Tonight Neil* it is genre which contributes most obviously to the tweaking of place. Its earliest origins were in my feeling that very few novels had been written about council estates, so place, to that extent, was unusually primary, for me, in my motives for writing it. Here was a setting which formed the background to the lives of millions of British people, and yet it was conspicuously absent from the literary form which is expected most comprehendingly to evoke those lives and to locate them in their most meaningful social context. I would agree to some extent with Salman Rushdie that British people don't understand their history because they don't understand that so much of its most crucial narrative happened outside Britain, but the contemporary novel seems to have taken this lesson so much to heart that it has gone to the opposite extreme, and the texts that are most admired tend to happen anywhere but Britain. Those that have a British setting are predominantly middle class, though that fact is rarely mentioned because class has become a very unfashionable subject.

Class and place have a crucial interaction in *Not Tonight Neil* because its setting is implicitly defined as one which the characters cannot escape, or, at least, have very little choice about. The novel as a form is preoccupied with money, and distinguishes itself from other forms in showing how money influences people's lives (Monty Python's cadging Scottish poet — 'Can you lend us a quid till Tuesday?' — shows how inappropriate the subject appears when versified). The interactions of money and setting are a constant preoccupation in Dickens and Austen and indicate again why place can never be objective in literature. Money facilitates travel but it more importantly introduces the possibility of choice of place, and a place will inevitably look and feel entirely different when choice is removed, as it generally is when your home is in a council estate in 1969, when no-one owned their properties there.

Generically, however, *Not Tonight Neil* mingles realism with a *whodunit* structure, and where realism is traditionally the mode which defines class and insists on the inescapability of money, the *whodunit* is more obviously textual and self-reflexive, and therefore calls realism into question. It is the character of Helen who

119

is the focus of the *whodunit* structure — very literally because it is her murder which drives that part of the narrative, but she is also an outsider where realism is concerned because she has defied class expectations by shunning her wealthy background in order to live with the working-class man who she loves. Her choice is similarly important for the novel's treatment of place. She spent part of her childhood in California, and she is multi-lingual, so she brings the possibility of other places into a setting which would otherwise be relentlessly focused on the council estate. Like the brief holiday visit to North Wales made by the narrator, Dennis Pugh, and his mum and dad, Helen's personifying of elsewhereness, provides relief from the singleness of setting and helps to define it by contrast.

Those muted contrasts aside, the novel's treatment of place is characterised by a self-conscious minimalism which is designed to illustrate the more generally minimal nature of the lives of my working-class characters. The focus is tightly restricted to a row of houses, stretches of grass in front of them, and a nearby collection of garages. There are significant times when the focus is even more rigid, when it is pointed intensely at a bedroom wall and its woodchip. This is the wall next to Dennis Pugh's bed, but it is also the wall next to the bed of Helen and Neil, the young couple next door, so it represents simultaneously a separation but also a surprisingly intimate and alarmingly illicit nearness. This image of the wall therefore represents, synecdochically, the cramped space occupied by the adolescent Dennis, and an intensity that arises from that crampedness: it is that combination which by implication has been formative for him and which therefore also influences his first-person narration. Narrowness and intensity are always the subtext when a single character is telling the story, but unreliability in this case is further exaggerated because Dennis is a cartoonist, and refers repeatedly to cartoon imagery. Throughout *Not Tonight Neil*, then, there is the further implication that place is being tweaked by reference to the caricatural vision of its narrator.

So cartoon and place is another key theme of the novel, and in this respect it is linked to my other work as a poet and critic. I have published two poetic sequences where cartoon plays a central role: in my Superman sequence, the superhero is invoked as a fantasy of extreme masculinity; my 'William Ewart Gladstone Strip' is spoken by a cartoonist who has been commissioned to construct a book that represents Victorian history.

The impact of time on place is another instability which fascinates me: *Not Tonight Neil* is set in 1969, and the council estate was then a very different place, objectively, to what it is now. My thinking in recent years has been influenced in this respect by the work of ecocritics like Lawrence Buell and postmodern geographers like Edward Soja and Doreen Massey who describes place and space as being

constructed out of the multiplicity of social relations across all spatial scales, from the global reach of finance and telecommunications, through the geography of the tentacles of national political power, to the social relations within the town, the settlement, the household and the workplace. It is a way of thinking in terms of the ever-shifting geometry of social/power relations, and it forces into view the real multiplicities of space-time.

[Doreen Massey, 1994. *Space, Place and Gender*. p. 4]

My personal experience of the contrasts between Mancunian Englishness and North Walian Welshness has drawn me towards this insistence on the problematic shiftingness of place and space, the insistence that each place is infiltrated by elsewhere. I'm fascinated by the way that the TV series *24* represents the interpenetration of places by setting itself in 'real time' (each hour-long episode represents a single hour in the narrative) and repeatedly resorting to a split screen to show the different actions which are taking place simultaneously in different locations. In *Not Tonight Neil*, the Manchester council estate in 1969 and Dennis's life in Chester in the early 1990s are placed in dialogue with each other. Time also alters the subjective perspective of those thinking about the past; it is not just that memory is distortive, but that the person who reflects on the past has altered in ways that have a significant relationship to the early development on which they reflect, and connected to that, to their place of origin.

The idea of the interpenetration of here and elsewhere, of a dialogue of places, made me want, after writing *Not Tonight Neil*, to write a novel where place would play a much more explicit role, and where it would resemble, as New York does in Toni Morrison's *Jazz*, another character. I had visited Cambodia, and Angkor Wat had astonished me, so I played with the idea of setting a novel in that country. But I was also interested in counter-factual history, and, contrastingly, in those novels which evoke real characters as David Peace does in *The Damned United*, and as Gordon Burn does in *Alma Cogan*, and I was sure that there would be fascinating possibilities in creating a narrative where a real person ended up living a very different life from the one that they actually lived.

I'm fascinated, also, by stand-up comedy, and thought that Peter Cook was a figure who created a range of possibilities as a character in a novel. So I set about researching Cook with the idea, at first, of writing about him in the way that David Peace had written about Brian Clough. One day, however, on a train travelling from Bangor to London, I had the idea of writing an alternative life for Peter Cook in which he dropped out of comedy and became a diplomat — which was the life his father had led, and for which Cook's public school, and then his modern languages degree at Cambridge, had prepared him. So I invented a narrative in which Peter Cook, in 1962, became a junior diplomat in the British embassy in Phnom Penh, where a key thematic point was that he was living a life which was 'out of place'. I made that phrase echo throughout the novel, in order to explore the idea of what might be perceived the appropriate life for someone to be living, and where they would live that life, and what, by contrast, would be inappropriate and therefore 'out of place'.

The biggest challenge in the novel was to write comedy for Peter Cook which was also 'out of place', which was created because he was living this variant life in a location far away from where he actually lived. You're sometimes told in a novel that a character is very witty, but given very few examples of that wit. Similarly, *Mad Men* is largely focused on the idea that the central character Don Draper is a genius of an adman, but the examples of his work are rare and, even then, amongst the least convincing parts of the TV series. With this novel, *The Crocodile Princess,* I wanted to attempt this audacious thing of writing lines for Peter Cook that were good enough for him to have invented, even if I was hedging that round with the point that when comic ideas are introduced into dialogue they are altered by the scene in which they're spoken and by interjections by people, in that scene, far less facilitating of them than Dudley Moore.

The Crocodile Princess is self-consciously fictive and its combination of truth and fiction is echoed in the last sentence of *The Crocodile Princess*: 'And that was partly true', which refers mostly to a specific remark at that point by one of the characters, but can also be applied to the novel as a whole. However, because the novel has a metafictional premise, it was all the more important that it have a strongly realist input so it not seem simply and easily fantastical. It was therefore important to me to do research into the life of a diplomat, and into 1962 as a historical moment, with the killing fields thirteen years in the future, and the powerful knowledge, in the present of 1962, of the ending of colonialism, and the oppressive presence of the Cold War. But the most important aspect of this realism was related to place — that Phnom Penh should be evoked in vivid detail, and it was here that I carried out the most painstaking research. I wanted to get precisely right the details about the climate, the timing of the dry season and the rainy season, and about the landscape, about where things are in relation to other things, like the 'rice road', for example, leading westwards out of Phnom Penh towards Battambang and the border with Thailand, and about the internal geography of Phnom Penh, with its spacious boulevards built on a French model, and its pastel-coloured buildings, and the invasion of riverine air from the waters flowing through and around it. Most important of all was the astonishing event in the Cambodian capital, when the Tonle Sap reverses the direction of its flow at the start of the rainy season: this is an actual occurrence, but it could easily be turned into a metaphor (Cook writes a song that refers to the river changing its mind) that is connected to the general theme of being 'out of place', and the general effect of systematic disorientation that I wanted above all to convey. (It also led to my own sense, when writing, that when I referred to Phnom Penh as a 'backwater' there was a pun somewhere behind it, though I doubt if that ever becomes apparent to the reader.)

I suppose that state of mind may well have a simple equivalent in my own sensibility which is related to my having no sense of direction at all. You might think that if I turned absent-mindedly out of a hotel room that I ought, fifty per cent of the time, to head in the right direction — so it's astonishing that I almost always go the wrong way. I've thought of writing a book called *Travels With No Sense Of Direction* because this lack does often have interesting results (as well as boring and frustrating ones). In Kurt Vonnegut's *Slaughterhouse Five*, Billy Pilgrim is said to come 'unstuck in time', but I have almost always, when I've travelled, at some point come unstuck in space. This may well have had an input into my having written a novel where only one of the main characters is from the place where it is set, and where all of them are lost in one sense or another.

That, too, is part of my core feeling that place cannot be divorced from cultural perspective: setting my novel in the diplomatic community in Phnom Penh means that its multiple perspectives are coloured politically as well as personally. But personal perspective is also crucial, and it's important for me that all the descriptions of the setting are filtered through individual characters. So my description of the Mekong is introduced in a way that means that it is not just describing the course of that major river, but also helping to define Edith Hartnell, who is one of the major characters:

Ever since her arrival in Cambodia, Edith Hartnell, the wife of the British Ambassador, had been drawn to the Buddhist idea of self-negation, but she often felt it as too easy, a dangerous temptation towards passive, submissive drift, especially because it was associated for her with an image of the Mekong river which sometimes arose in her so powerfully that it threatened altogether to overwhelm her sense of self. Repeatedly she thought of how completely the river could change itself, of how it fell ten metres in the dry season, so that it looked subdued and depressed where stony reefs and islands pushed up out of it, but roared back again when the rains flooded into it and swirled with currents that coiled and spiralled and were heavy with silt and carried bottles and broken trees and the corpses of pigs and dogs and water buffaloes. Edith lost herself watching these changes then recalling them as she drifted off at night into sleep: for some months she had been plagued by nightmares and she had chosen to contemplate the Mekong, at first, as a calming image. So she had deliberately imagined, step by step, its course, from its origins as a trickle out of a Tibetan glacier in the Himalayas, identifying with its gradual, relentless growth as it was joined by mountain streams and melting snow, identifying with its changes as the land around it, in south-western China between Burma and Thailand, altered, so it plunged down steep gorges. A river, like a person is transformed by its surroundings, so she then identified with its new, warmer self in the borders of Laos where it flowed through the hills and jungle vegetation, falling further into Cambodia through a series of rapids, and slowing as it entered southern Vietnam and then wandered past Saigon into the South China Sea.

Filtering objective truths about the Mekong, in this way, through the point of view of one of the characters, is representative of how I always want to treat place in all of my writing: this passage indicates how this major river is thoroughly altered by culture and subjectivity because it evokes the way that the Mekong has entirely infiltrated Edith's sensibility. Just as both a river and a person are changed by their surroundings, both are changed by their mutual interaction.

A Sort of Gravity
Mark Charlton

Twenty years ago we took a holiday to the Beara peninsula, the most remote of the three fingers of land, reaching out to the Atlantic on the South West tip of Eire. It was March, and the boys were small.

Actually, that's not quite right. Daniel was a toddler; Mike was still kicking his mother's belly and wouldn't come screaming into our world for another three months.

Quite why I'd suggested we visit Beara I can't remember.

I think it was the idea of being on the edge, beyond the tourist trails. I had notions of brittle skies and windswept bays; walking on the cliffs in the day, and of nights drinking whisky and Guinness in bars thick with smoke. It would be romantic, I'd said to Jane, and cosy too.

As it turned out, it was bitter. And in March, largely closed.

My abiding memory is the two days Jane and I spent in bed, so sick with food poisoning we took turns, between vomiting, to feed and change Daniel. I remember lying on the sofa, as he crawled round our rented bungalow, rain seeping through the inadequate seals of the patio doors.

But perhaps I have that wrong too.

For it's entirely possible I'm confusing the events with something that happened another time — and that what I'm doing is to remember remembering, years of which morph the details, like Chinese whispers, such that the only 'truth', which remains, is a recollected feeling. A feeling more certain than any chronology or facts.

A lingering sense of place.

Eighteen years later and Daniel is hovering in the kitchen for longer than usual, a piece of toast in one hand, a Kit-Kat in the other.

He stuffs the latter in his pocket and turns to me. 'They say there's a Goldilocks zone for universities.'

He bites the bread and continues to mumble.

'Not so far that you don't get away, but near enough to bring home your washing.'

I ponder this as he opens the fridge, examines a block of Wensleydale and casually breaks off a chunk.

'Where did you hear this?'

'School'.

For Daniel this is quite a reveal. He's not spoken much about his university choices and I wonder what he wants to tell me, so I probe.

'How far does this zone extend?'

'Between a hundred and two hundred miles. Most of my friends are looking at Cardiff or Reading — those sorts of places.'

'And you?'

'It depends on my offers.'

'Of course, but where would you most like to go?'

He glances at me and reaches for a packet of biscuits.

'Well?' I ask.

'What?'

'Well, where in this Goldilocks zone are you thinking of going?'

'I'm not,' he replies, stuffing the biscuits in his bag and heading to the hall. 'I want to be more independent.'

There's a blast of air as the kitchen door swings and the front one slams.

'Newcastle!'

Daniel has confirmed his decision.

'You want to go to Newcastle?'

I visualise a line a map but know already that aside from Scotland, it's the furthest place from home he could have chosen.

Later that morning, I wonder if Falmouth might be a longer trip by road and consult Google Maps — the distance doesn't compare.

Newcastle.

Of all the places...

The artist Terry Frost once said that the images he painted in later life were first formed as long as fifty years previous. They were a response, he said, to places that had lain not so much dormant, as maturing in his mind. It took time for these to resolve, for feelings to clarify and truth to emerge.

Of all the holidays we have taken, that trip to Beara is the one we groan about most. And yet there's seldom a week goes by when I don't recall a man I met there. He spoke to me in a crowded pub, commenting that in Ireland I shouldn't be drinking Scotch — his cultured north American accent, at odds with a filthy jacket.

As we chatted, he told me he'd emigrated to Canada as young man, living there for fifty years before returning to Beara in his seventies.

Why had he come home?

'Because we're drawn back,' he explained, 'by a slow but insistent yearning.' He'd returned, he said, not to die, though he knew that was coming — but because it was necessary — because, for all he'd lived away, he'd never really left.

Approaching the Tyne from the south, the A1 takes a turn to the west. It arcs beneath the Angel of the

North, descending slowly to the valley proper. On the far bank, the rows and squares of Newcastle's urban sprawl rise like theatre stalls.

Daniel is consulting the map. 'The directions say we need to go through Gateshead.'

I ignore him and carry on.

'We'll take the Scotswood Bridge and come in by the Vickers factory,' I say. I know what I'm doing.

The carriageway continues to arc, crossing the Tyne on a high viaduct, and I spot the old bridge below us.

'Shit.'

Daniel tosses the map to one side and there follows a few minutes of cursing as I reorientate my sense of direction.

The viaduct isn't new — it's been there thirty years — and yet somehow it feels that way. We get off at the next roundabout and make our way to the river at the industrial suburb of Elswick.

Growing up on Tyneside we looked at the river as a social divide. I wouldn't have used those words then, but as children we considered our cousins, who lived in Gateshead, to come from somewhere much lesser — as if they'd come down in the world.

The same held true along its course — Tynemouth, we regarded as better than South Shields; Wallsend was better than Jarrow — Northumberland (as Tyne and Wear was then) a much, much, better place than County Durham. There's an element of bias in this — shaped by the limited familiarity and territories that are our childhoods — but there is also some truth.

Gateshead plays second fiddle to its grander neighbour, and broadly, as you trace the river, the northern bank has the edge in wealth and facilities. You see much the same pattern in other regional centres:

Newport's relationship to Cardiff, for example; Birkenhead's to Liverpool.

But in truth, I've never lived in Newcastle at all. I grew up by the coast, in what we thought of (wrongly) as an altogether smarter place. My junior school overlooked the North Sea — its cold horizon was a constant presence. Grey waves and a biting wind are what defined my childhood landscape.

Newcastle was where my father worked, at least before his breakdown. He hated the place; refused to drive there; always shopped in Sunderland. As children, Newcastle was a rare day out; as teenagers, a rite of passage to go alone. Later, when I returned from university, it would become my place of work too — though soon after, I moved further north, as near to the hills as my job would allow.

Now I think about it, I wanted to be more independent.

But it's near to impossible to live or work in the North East without an affinity to the *Toon*. The city dominates the region: its landmarks, its culture, the football team... Even my father was proud of its heritage.

And thirty years since I left, occasionally someone will comment, 'That accent of yours; you're not a Geordie are you?'

We'd been chatting all day on the slow journey north. Daniel had talked about his course, about the seven years it takes to qualify as an architect.

I'd recalled my time as a student; suggested the experience hadn't changed much, and sensed a disbelief in the politeness of his replies.

I wanted him to enjoy it, I said. There's too much worry about debt and fees and what comes of it all. University, I told him, was a comprehensive education

— I'd be disappointed if he didn't get pissed in his first few days.

That shouldn't be a problem, he'd laughed.

But I knew the banter was distraction on my part.

Daniel is our eldest son and the first to leave home.

Jane couldn't face the trip.

'It's only twelve weeks to Christmas,' he'd reassured her.

She'd hugged him before we left, her face streaked with tears.

I had to peel her arms from his neck.

As we approach the City I'm alert to its changes: the new car parks and pub signs, an out of town shopping and cinema complex — the evolution of regeneration and decay. Whole districts are missing: some, because I'm misremembering; others, I realise, as we pass an urban slag heap, are being demolished. There's a new green at Cruddas Park, where once stood the *Likely Lads'* high rise flats.

But for all the changes, the macro geography is the same — this is unmistakably the western approach to Newcastle: the river on my right, the afternoon sun dipping behind me. In half a mile we'll drop to the station, hang a left at Collingwood Street and take the ring road to the University. The familiarity is tangible, and as we reach the end of Scotswood Road I'm humming the Blaydon Races.

'We turn in a moment,' interrupts Daniel.

He's retrieved the directions and is consulting the map.

I'm planning on ignoring him a second time when the traffic is forced sharp left. The road is simultaneously familiar and new — its angles are all wrong, we're at the rear of buildings instead of the front. I scan for reference points — not so much lost, as temporarily disoriented.

A taxi hoots me as I pause.

The diversion brings us to St James' Park, the city's secular cathedral. Daniel comments on its 'inside out' architecture, how the angular scaffolding is a kind of homage to the region's industrial heritage; the glass palisade and steel pillars, he says, have a gladiatorial echo.

His perspective interests me. The last time I was here the stadium was a concrete toilet, the Gallowgate end an open terrace and the streets around it thick with menace. Today, it feels hopeful, and a statement of pride — a welcome of sorts.

We come to the Haymarket and the Civic Centre. It's classic Sixties and as if it too were a cathedral, there's a verdigris tower, crowned with twelve seahorse heads. I tell Daniel how the portico has a dome shaped ceiling, which if you shout load enough, will echo at middle C.

Daniel's halls are somewhere near. They're a tower block, next to the old Polytechnic, in the centre of a one-way system. I can see them, but can't figure out how to reach the access road.

We pass the Hancock museum, get lost in Leazes Park and find our way back to New Bridge Street. This happens twice and each time Daniel gets increasingly fractious. But despite the traffic, I'm uncharacteristically calm. I'm drinking it in, almost disappointed when he cries, 'We're here — turn left now!'

A marshal in a high-viz jacket guides us to a bay.

I cut the engine and just for a moment we sit together, the windscreen misting as we each hold our thoughts.

Inside Daniel's room, I take a photo to show Jane — he's standing by the door, wearing the jacket she'd bought him, looking lost and vulnerable. There's a wardrobe that's awkwardly placed next to the sink, and what appear to be a number of water pipes, diverted through a duct on the wall. The paintwork is spotted where posters have been removed.

I start tapping the pipes.

'Stop that Dad.'

'I'm just checking. You don't want a room that vibrates every time someone goes to the toilet. And look at these walls, if I were you, I'd ask to have them repainted.'

'It's fine, Dad.'

'You're paying thousands to stay here. You might as well get it right; why don't we go down to the reception and…'

'I said it's fine! I don't care about the pipes.'

We're interrupted by a knock on the door.

Two students are delivering leaflets. The one who speaks has a soft Northumbrian lilt, more throaty than Tyneside; I reckon he's from Blyth. 'We're organising a pub crawl tomorrow,' he explains. 'It costs a tenner but you get a voucher for five pints. We finish at the Quayside; that's the best part of town, like'.

'Is this your Dad?' He calls to me over Daniel's shoulder, 'You can come n'all if you buy the shots!'

I surprise him by replying, '*Ye divn't want me alang, I was gannin to the Big Market lang before ye were born.*'

Daniel shifts awkwardly as they hand him a leaflet

'I'll bear it in mind,' he says. 'I've only just arrived.'

The promoters move on and Daniel closes the door. He looks unsure what to do or say. I snap him again with the phone.

'How about we walk into town and grab a bite, then I'll leave you to it?'

135

'That would be great,' he smiles.

As we're leaving I slip him some cash. 'That's a bit extra for fresher's week. You find those lads and book a place on that night out while I pop to the *netty*. I'm going to check if those pipes rattle when I flush.'

'Alright,' he smiles.

'You mean, *ahrlreet*,' I tease him. 'You're not in Wales now, son.'

It's only minutes to the town. I plan a route in my mind and stride towards the centre.

Passing the City Halls I tell Daniel of their famous Lindisfarne concerts. I think there's a swimming baths next door — there is; they're closed. We carry on to Northumberland Street and at the entrance to Eldon Square I sense again that disjunction of the familiar and the new.

Except by now I'm enjoying it — every shop is a delight, every poster something to comment on. There's a golden sky, flecked with starlings and I'm walking briskly, running a commentary, as much to myself as to Daniel.

We pass a Gregg's bakery — *they started here you know, bet they sell stotty cakes.* At Fenwick's department store — *it was the first ever of those; once most profitable store in the UK.* Then Marks & Spencer's — *they used to open on Sundays for the Norwegian ferries.*

At the junction of Blackett Street I turn right by the fancy Northern Jewellers; round the corner is Grey's monument, the Theatre Royal, the Grainger Market. Newcastle centre is impressive by any standard — its Georgian buildings are made of sandstone — solid, mercantile; intensely Northern.

The bars are filling on Grey Street. I take a right down an alley —*some good pubs here* — there are bouncers on the doors and the drinkers are queuing to get in. We carry on to the Big Market. Daniel is trailing behind so I wait for him to reach me.

'If we go up here, we'll come to Mark Toney's — *great place for ice cream* — then we can cut past the cathedral and down to the station. There's the tunnel that heads to the Bridge Pub where they do real ale and folk music…'

Daniel's phone rings.

'Hello Mum.'

He tells her he's settled into his room. 'We're somewhere in the town and heading to a bridge that does real ale… Yes, I'm fine… Dad's talking Geordie and having a nostalgia-fest.'

'I am not having a nostalgia-fest,' I say indignantly when he's finished the call

'No,' he laughs, 'that would be like you at all.'

I had dreaded Daniel leaving.

When he chose Newcastle I told him there would be logistical problems; no chance of coming home during term. What about that Goldilocks zone?

He wanted to branch out, he said.

I understood, but in a sense that made it worse.

Friends we spoke to were less troubled. Some couldn't wait for their kids to leave — it was the start of a new phase they said, an opportunity for both to move on. And in any case, they'd be back soon enough — scrounging in the holidays, bringing back their mates.

Jane said they were right; that I shouldn't project my past on Daniel.

But we're shaped by our memories.

When I left for university my parents divorced. I wasn't sad about that, they should have parted long before. Soon after, my grandfather died — or did that happen first? It doesn't matter. The important point is I had no 'home' to come back to. I'd felt crushingly alone.

But even that is part fiction. For at eighteen, I couldn't wait to leave and had no intention of returning. University was a coming of age; I was bereft when it ended. A few months ago, I was contacted by the alumni office — they'd read my book and were interviewing former students. Thirty years since I graduated, I said, I'd not entirely left it behind.

And the fact is, I did return to Tyneside. There were three million unemployed in 1982, and the North East wasn't exactly the logical choice — but I was drawn back, by the idea of it as much as anything — by a sort of gravity.

In the event, I stumbled on a job, bought my first house (as you could do then) and began that journey of chance and choices which shapes all our futures. The other week I realised it's more than half my life since I'd moved to Wales, and yet those two places — opposite coasts — are inextricably linked in my personal landscape.

'I wish it were simpler,' I'd said to Jane.

In the weeks before Daniel left, I'd wake at night — torn between a yearning to hold on, and the counter knowledge, that for him to flourish, I had to let go.

The Crown Pasada is one of those city pubs with a long bar, brass rails and a line of hand pumps. We find a seat in a booth that's edged with green leather benches and squeeze in by a couple — the woman gives me a smile.

'This is one of the oldest pubs on the quayside,' I explain to Daniel. 'We used to come here after work.'

I sit back and take in the surroundings; the bar is filling fast. There's a stained glass window above the booth, a mêlée of drinkers, dressed for the night. I reach for my beer and spill a little on the table.

'Go careful with that,' says the woman who'd smiled.

She is slim with long blonde hair, wearing jeans and a white lace blouse; she's probably forty-something but looks a little younger. 'You out for the night?' she asks.

'My son's come to university today; I'm showing him the town?'

She glances at Daniel, 'What's he studying?'

'Architecture.'

'That's a long course.' She's drains an oversized glass of white wine. 'You'll be coming back often then.'

'I'm not sure about that.'

'But you're from round here, aren't you?'

'I was — a long time ago.'

Her companion seems ill at ease, he's suggesting they leave. But she wants another drink, and after a hissed exchange he heads to the bar.

She asks me where I'd lived.

'I was brought up in Cullercoats.'

'Really. What school did you go to?'

The directness of the question takes me back. I look at her carefully. She's pretty — high cheek bones — a bit older than I'd thought. I'm wondering if I know her?

'I went to Rockcliffe.'

'That's in Whitley Bay.'

She was right — my mother had taught there.

'I live on the Broadway,' she told me. 'Do you know it?'

They're three deep at the bar and her chap is caught in the throng; he's looking in our direction, shrugging his shoulders and trying to catch her attention. She sees this, but ignores him and asks about where I live now

We talk about Wales. I say that in many ways it's like the North East — the people, the castles; much of the landscape. Except in the west, the sun sets over the sea

'That's a strange thing to mention.'

139

I told her I was a writer; that I'd planned to go back to Cullercoats tomorrow. It was a notion I'd been fostering, an idea for my next book. 'My uncle still lives there,' I said. Perhaps I'd call in to see him

'I should give you my number,' she replied

Daniel, who could hear all this, nudged me in the ribs. Shouldn't we be heading back; we'd not had anything to eat

'There's an Italian on Dean Street,' I suggested.

'I need the toilet first,' he said.

The blonde woman was talking again to her companion. They were having a row but I couldn't hear above the din. She turned her back and he stood up angrily, pushing his way through the crowd

'Don't bother about him,' she said. 'He's in a huff because I'm talking to you. Has your son gone back to his digs?'

'He's at the loo. We're grabbing a pizza, then I'll leave him to it.

'Are you staying over?'

'At his hall,' I lied.

'You're worried about him leaving him aren't you?

'It's not so much that; it's whether he'll come back.'

'The thing to remember, is that we all do the end.' She paused to finish her drink. 'Look at that little squirt who just left me. He'll be waiting outside I expect.

I could smell the alcohol on her breath; her eyes were struggling to focus

'Are you going to be alright?' I asked

'I think you're lovely,' she said

And with that, she leant over and pulled my head firmly towards her — her lips tasted of wine and lipstick

I prised myself away, just as Daniel returned

'Welcome home,' she whispered.

'What was up with that woman?' Daniel asked.

We'd given up on somewhere to eat and were heading back through town.

'I think she was pissed — she tried to snog me when you went to the loo.'

He laughed. 'Wait till I tell Mum.'

'Don't you dare!'

I'd bet if you asked him now, he'd not remember, but as we walked to my hotel he put his arm round my shoulder and steadied me.

'Remember, you can fly home anytime. I'll pay for the flights and collect you at the airport.'

'Thanks.'

'Or maybe me and your mum can come up — and your brothers. Dylan can stay with us and Mike could crash at your place?'

'Sure.'

'I could show you Northumberland. There are castles and moorland, and some brilliant coast — it's not like Wales of course but…'

'It's alright Dad. You do know, I'm going to miss you — and I appreciate all you've done.'

We'd reached my hotel.

'Send me a text when you get to your halls?'

'Sure.'

I hugged him goodbye; smelled his hair as he pulled away.

'Are you going home tomorrow?' he called.

'Of course — where else?'

'I meant to the coast, for your book — like you said to that woman?'

'No — I don't need to go now.'

'That's good,' he smiled.

And I didn't.

There's a style of writing about place that I've come to mistrust.

It's prevalent in much of the 'new nature' genre, though is common with travel writers too. Typically, it involves the author visiting a 'wild' or remote location; usually they are undertaking a journey or quest of sorts. Not only are they outsiders, but the place they describe is new to them.

And from this flimsy platform, these authors present the landscape and the natural world as a means to deeper knowledge, an understanding of the self.

I don't buy it.

For no matter how immaculately phrased — and make no mistake, their writing is often beautiful — it is a chimera. Occasionally there's a *volta-esque* insight, but more often the 'place' is used as a prop to support the presentation of copious research. Indeed, the presence of background material, though not definitive, is a fairly reliable warning that the work will be thin on authenticity.

This is harsh, and unapologetically Romantic in its view of what the best writing on place should be. But it seems to me there a there are no short cuts; that a deep response takes time and presence.

This returned to me recently, when I bought a house in France. It's a retirement dream, a lifetime's ambition, built on thirty years of visiting the Haute Savoir. As the purchase progressed, the idea of it grew in my mind, consuming me for months — like a child nearing Christmas I was counting the 'sleeps' to the day.

And yet when I finally took possession, I felt hollow. The village was cold; empty of connection. Jane was beside herself with worry. 'The house is too big,' I said. 'I've made a colossal mistake.'

It has taken months to come round — slowly at that — and significantly, it is time in the mountains, reconnecting with the places and memories I hold dear, which has helped the most. I have learned again, what ought to have been obvious — that we can't 'buy' place, or a resonance to it. It has to be earned — through experience and sweat; through joys and failures.

My near neighbour in Wales is John Knapp Fisher*, one of our finest landscape painters. The vast majority of his lifetime's work draws on the few square miles running from his cottage to the sea. In an echo of my return to the Tyne, he travels regularly to the Thames, where over eighty years ago, he was born and brought up.

The writing I trust, and which I want to create, is something akin to his paintings. It is fuelled by a response that comes from years of attention — in the case of wild places, from having walked and watched and loved in the landscape; in the case of the urban, much the same.

John's paintings are never strictly accurate. When I wrote the piece about Newcastle I could have consulted maps, ensured the street names were correct, double checked the 'facts'. But I didn't, and I haven't since — because it doesn't matter. And more importantly, to change them now would diminish the response. I'm not certain if Fenwick's really was the 'first ever department store', or if the town hall ceiling 'resonates at Middle C'. The point is that we believed it at the time — it was part of our myth, our idea of the City.

The inner story of my return to Newcastle is not yet complete. There is more to explore about the pull of home and the places we apply that name to. More too, about the letting go and holding on to those we love; the mash-up of people and place and memory which makes for a richly lived life.

One of the challenges, but also the joys, of being a writer, is that the very act of choosing our words — no matter how inadequate they may be — requires us to respond to our feelings. And this is as vital to any description of 'place' as it is to relationships, or personal journeys or for that matter religious epiphany.

To write fully of place we must look 'in' more than we do 'out'.

Before I was a writer I used to paint.

Once, I visited an exhibition by Rose Wylie, whose work at first sight resembles the slapdash rendering of a child. I couldn't fathom what the fuss was about, what her oversize canvasses were saying? But I found myself returning, looking time and again at the directness and intensity of the images. Wylie captures those domestic moments, which burn into our consciousness; that we instantly forget and yet, hold onto for a lifetime.

If a 'sense of place' is the connection between the landscape and the self, then central to it, must surely be memory — both recollected and subconscious. So too must be fallibility, because our deepest memories are just that — images made icons, and all the more so with every photo and story and the version of truth we tell ourselves.

I write always in the first person and seldom venture into fiction, finding it difficult to take on the character of another. This is a preference, rather than a statement of what's correct — I'm aware it's a huge limitation. To find new perspectives, I sometimes write notes 'from my past'; occasionally I'll imagine looking back on the present.

When I studied for a degree in creative arts, I was given an assignment to write in the voice of a child. This is astonishingly difficult and there are few writers who do it well. Harper Lee's *To Kill a Mocking Bird* is often quoted, but for me (and I can't quite believe I'm saying this) it fails – at least, Scout's voice is not like any child I've met. Young children, like Wylie's paintings, are truer to their nature. Give them a crayon and they'll draw their whole experience, not just the visual world.

As adults our responses are more complex, taking time to resolve. I like to revisit. Indeed, returning is one of my greatest joys; I delight too in the familiar, have no desire to travel widely and am skeptical that it broadens the mind. All these are preferences, but it helps to declare them.

Occasionally I use photographs as prompts to my writing. But if I do, I will angle and fragment the prints, cutting and pasting cheap digital copies, so they become evocations rather than a coherent or singular memory. I've learned not to be precious about note taking; my sketchbooks are full of shopping lists, household measurements and the doodles of my boys. These things are all part of the places we were at.

Returning to painting, I am tempted to offer the challenge set by my old tutor — you should draw the taste of ice cream, he said! It's an exercise that confronts the idea of painting as illustration, requiring us to consider how our 'experience' is greater than simply what we see. Unsurprisingly, young children don't find it so hard!

I'm conscious that I'm talking here of approaches more than offering a workshop exercise — but then I'm skeptical of those too. There's a danger they become a form in themselves — short enough to be read aloud, a subtle twist, occasional pathos — but nearly always rather shallow.

Responding more fully to the connections between self and place is tough, and the outcome always imperfect. It seems to me that patience is essential, for

145

yet more research will yield only yet more facts — when what's important, is a different sort of truth.

To be a writer is always to struggle with form and feeling. There's no correct way to begin, just as there's no escaping the long hours at the keyboard. The important thing is to try and say something worthwhile — and we achieve that most often, when we're true to ourselves.

Sadly, John Knapp Fisher died in February 2015, shortly after I wrote this piece. Though not close friends, I knew him well enough to call by at his cottage. John could articulate his ideas with a rare clarity. He was also confident in what he created and how he worked — an inspirational reminder that one of the challenges, in writing or in painting, is first to find our strengths, and then to trust them.

A Landscape Mass
in Three Movements
Jim Perrin

1: Gloria

Place as Chorus? Venues that resonate with our lives' stories?

We may choose to view place as fixed entity, yet its role
— in our lives, in the reports and fictions our alembic
minds distil from the juices of experience — is more as
sounding-board, before which we stand to preach, to
others and to ourselves, of character, its growth, its
resonance.

Place is — or at least was, before Program Era and
UEA orthodoxies and all their metro-lit adherents and
cheer-leaders rendered it inadmissible superfluity — the
great commonplace of British fiction. It dominated the
mise en scene of every major novel. From Scott, George
Eliot and the Brontes to Dickens and Hardy, E.M
Forster, James Joyce, D.H. Lawrence and Henry
Williamson, the settings through which a character
moves are as memorable as the characters themselves,
reflecting emotionally, culturally and intellectually upon
them.

When I set to composing the long novella, 'The
Burning', with which my Cinnamon story collection (*A
Snow Goose and other Utopian Fictions*, 2014) more or less
concludes, what was uppermost in my mind was the
interplay between these people my imagination had
come to know, and the landscape they would inhabit,
with all its associative texture, story and community, its
history and archetypal mirrorings. Myth-taken identities!
In a sense, as writers we invent nothing and imagine

very little. We merely collate, view afresh, re-order, introduce, contemplate likely outcome, whilst all the time the eternal commonplaces of human character assert themselves.

So here are my Bryn and Bethan, accommodating themselves to the dimensions of Cwm Blaen-yr-Afon and its society. I know these two young people well. The park-keeper of Cwm Donkin said to the returning poet, 'I've known him — I've known him by the thousand!' And I know this place too — have known it the greater part of my life, can see it now through the long perspectives. As Joan Didion puts it, 'We tell ourselves stories to go on living' — even if it is vicariously, through those we have summoned to the co-operative enterprise with a reader which is page-life.

From 'The Burning' in *A Snow Goose and other Utopian Fictions*:

"It was a week later when Bethan and Bryn walked across the valley from Porthaur one bright evening and climbed up the path that led through old slate workings to level pastures around Tanybwlch.

'Eleri said there were turfs cut and stacked to dry round the side of the barn', Bethan told Bryn as they retrieved the key and opened the door into the tiny, quarry-tiled hall, a room leading off on either side and the stairs straight ahead. 'I've never had a peat fire,' she said, in response to the damp and musty air that enveloped them.

'They're not very exciting, not much in the way of flames,' Bryn replied, 'but they smell wonderful — better even than woodsmoke. I'll bring some in and we can get it lit.'

He put the big rucksack down in the parlour, she deposited hers alongside, and he went out to fetch curling brown rectangles of hard dry turf, stacking them by the hearth before going back to fetch kindling from the barn. Soon blue skeins of smoke were drifting out of the chimney, rising into the still evening, scenting the air with a sharp redolence. Bryn filled the old black kettle at the spring, set it on the trivet and swivelled it round above the low flames.

'Hope you don't mind a bit of rust in your tea — Mam used to say it was good for anaemia. It'll take forever to boil. We could go out for a walk whilst we're waiting.'

He built up the fire and they walked across the moor behind the house, following a lead through heather to the summit tors of Mynydd Craig Goch.

'Look, Bryn — you can see two seas. You can see forever! Those hills right down to the south, where are they? And what's that line across the horizon against the sunset? It looks like more mountains?'

'Those are the Wicklow hills in Ireland, and the ones to the south are Mynydd Preseli. And can you see that last bump on the peninsula? That's Ynys Enlli — there's a well in the cliff on the landward side of the sound with ancient carved steps down to sea-level and then you have to climb across the rock. It was the holiest place in all Wales to the old pilgrims, three journeys there equivalent to one to Rome. You can see the entire pilgrim route from up here. See where it crosses the sands from Llanfihangel y Traethau, out from the Cob that we drove across? They needed guides for that crossing. And there are the churches and wells all along the peninsula. I'd like to walk that route one day, busking with my guitar and taking what chance and charity came my way.' He turned to her: 'And now you've

149

come my way, and everything's a hundred times better because I can do it with you.'

She kissed him, her eyes shining, then turned from him and asked, 'What's that down there, that valley with the big slate-tips, all shadowy and leading up towards the big pointy hill?'

'That's Dyffryn Nantlle, and if you look over there, you see that long straight coastline running north, and a rock with the tide breaking round it half- a-mile off-shore? That's Caer Arianrhod. There's a long story, very old, begins there about Gwydion the enchanter, and Lleu Llaw Gyffes, and Blodeuedd the woman Gwydion made from flowers for Lleu . But she was *heb cydwybod* — without conscience — and she betrayed him, so Gwydion turned her into Blodeuwedd, the flower-faced one, the owl...'

The long quaver of a tawny owl rose out of the woods and travelled to them across the heather. Bethan moved close to Bryn. She was shivering, put her arms round him for warmth and reassurance: 'It's so powerful, this country of yours, Bryn, with its stories and memories. I can understand why my parents ran away, but it's what is drawing me back. That and you — you're the enchanter for me, not Gwydion down at Cwrt y Cadno, though I like him, for all that he's daft and funny and talks about nothing but Greaves scramblers and the best drench for *llynghyren.*'

'Your accent's coming on, Beth! Where did you learn that word from? It's the proper one, too — mostly we just call it *y fflwc.*'

'Aunt Eleri sent me down to the vet's in Chwilog to pick up some drench this morning to treat the rams in the bottom pasture — she rehearsed me in how to ask for it in Welsh. But I still had to

150

bluff my way and get by with nods and smiles when the girl spoke back. She must have thought I was a complete idiot, one of those products of a marriage between cousins you were telling me about. I hope Auntie Angharad's not discovered we are related after all. I'd hate to be pregnant with the fear of what that might cause hanging over me. Not that I'm planning on having any babies just yet, of course, but it would be so gorgeous having a little Bryn with dark curly hair running around. I'll get along to the family planning when I'm back in London and start on the pill …'

'Good,' said Bryn, looking fondly at her, 'We need a few years to ourselves first. How long have we known each other now — not quite ten days?'

'You mean you can't remember the exact day, hour and minute when we first met..?'

They set off down from the summit.

'You can see everything in Cwm Blaenyrafon from up here as well,' said Bethan. 'Look, there by the sheep-pens above Porthaur — that's Mabon's car isn't it? And he's watching through binoculars. How weird!'

They ran down to the house, where the kettle was now boiling with a high singing note. Bethan made tea whilst Bryn placed more turfs carefully on the fire, primed and lit a Tilley lamp and hung it hissing from a hook on the beam. They took their cups outside for a last look down into the valley, across which the shadow of the ridge was spreading fast.

'Bryn, he's still there!'

She pointed again to the concrete-block pens above Porthaur. There was the yellow car parked alongside, and the quick flash of light as the hunched figure standing by it swung his binoculars round, and the last rays of the sun streaming through the bwlch caught their lenses and sent their reflection back like flying sparks, before in a quick instant the shadow of the hill enveloped and quenched them."

I know this cottage. Its walls are cracked now, slates missing from the roof, all hovers on the edge of ruin. An old woman lived here fifty years ago, alone, her story barely remembered now — a story from which the few details I can recall resonate so clearly. As, returning to our story, does this incident —that happened...

*

"In the first silvery light of morning they climbed again to the ridge, set off along it with rucksacks on their backs. At the drystone obelisk on Mynydd Tal-y-Mignedd they sat down to rest with their backs to the pillar and their faces to the east, where the sun was etching the bulk of Snowdon hard against the pale blue of the sky. The ridge of Y Lliwedd was reddening, and suddenly the great orb of flame lifted clear of it and illuminated the slopes, turned the valley-mists pink, and raced along the saurian ridge to light up their faces.

'I suppose I shall have to think of going back to London soon, but leaving you and leaving here is going to be so hard now.'

'You'll be back. We can work hard to make the time pass. I'll be here for you.'

'Will you, Bryn?' She turned to him, eyes glistening.

'For as long as you want me, I'll be here. You're magical to me too, Beth. I want no-one but you. At first sight — Aunt Eleri says without an element of that you can forget it. I knew when I saw you running down the path to the abbey. There was a poem came straight into my mind — want to hear some of it? It's by the bastard son of a twelfth-century prince. Welsh first, then I'll translate — and just three lines, because I can't remember all of it.'

'Stop teasing and get on with it — foreplay's one thing, but a girl likes to be ravished eventually, you know. She likes her man inside her, and not fretting around in the cold showing off how much he knows.'

Dewis gennyf i di; beth yw gennyd di fi?
Beth a dewi di, deg ei gosteg?
Dewisais i fun fal nad atreg gennyf.'

'It's got my name in there, twice. What does it mean? It's so musical.'

'He's telling her that she's his choice, and asking how he stands in her affections, and why she's silent, beautiful silence that she is, and telling himself that he's chosen a girl of whom he'll never repent — and I feel all that about you, Beth."'

Infatuation's what's going on here — between two young people; for a landscape; with a language. There is an element of autobiographical underpinning. I am remembering a time from over forty years ago in my own life. The characters here, even their conversation, are closely based on the people I knew in a community at that time. We adapt the matter of our own experience, the circumstances of our own lives, to weave the fabric of fiction. More from their story:

"They circled on round to Mynydd Drws-y-Coed. The sky to the north-west was darker now and a wind rising. Looking out towards the sea they watched luminous grey columns of rain drifting and swaying towards the land. 'We'll follow the edge of the forestry down to the pass, and then we can go

153

along the old tramway back to Cwrt y Cadno, but it looks like we're going to get wet!'

They reached the pass as the rain started, heavy drops blotching the stones. A thick bank of mist enveloped them, annihilating the landscape. Hand in hand they launched down a steep slope of wet slate-scree that moved beneath their feet and around them, clattering and slithering away. One sinister-shaped block, freed from its resting place, bounded past as if in slow motion, turned on end at the limit of visibility, hung for a moment and then disappeared into space. Moments later a crash echoed up from far beneath as it hit bottom.

The edge of a deep quarry-hole was only feet away from them. A squall of hail hissed across the slope. They traversed crab-like and terrified, Bryn beneath Bethan to guard against a slip and reassure, across the lip of the void to reach the old incline, scrambled on to it, and were soon descending out of the clouds into sunlight again and the green belvedere of the tramway that led them along the valley-side, back past the top barn and along to the path down to Porthaur.

'Let's drop the rucksacks, get into dry clothes and have some breakfast,' Bryn said. 'That was an adventure! You get these squalls in the hills in spring. Are you O.K. Beth? You were wonderful up there — so calm and sensible.'

'Well I didn't feel like that, Mister Bryn, I can tell you! I was terrified. And that hole appearing out of nowhere! Anyway, I'm just a bit wet, that's all, so let's go get dry and fed before we see them all at Cwrt y Cadno.'

A couple of hours later, scrambled eggs and toast and coffee eaten and their wet clothes drying on the line, they made their way through the fields towards Cwrt y Cadno, parting by the gate as Bryn headed up to join the boys. In the kitchen Eleri poured tea for Beth. 'Just made, *cariad*! There you go. This little one's getting lively, look. She's been sleeping with Nell in her basket this last couple of nights, curled up together. No more warming oven for her! And look at the weight she's put on.'

The orphan lamb followed Eleri's every move, snickering after her and kicking its feet up in comic dances across the slate floor.

'It's funny the way Nell is with her. I've seen it with sheepdog bitches before, but not often. The little one, see, she's been suckling at her — just like men, these tiny lambs, any tit will do and no conscience. Sometimes the bitch will come into milk, too. They're a queer bundle of psycho-chemical responses, the creatures that inhabit this earth, *cariad*, and we're no different.'

Bethan told her about the smell of burning peat and being on the hill-tops in the sunset and dawn, about the sudden squall and the frightening descent, about Mabon watching them from the valley. Eleri's grey eyes were amused, intent, concerned at the last. 'I don't like the sound of that, *cariad*. He's had — what would you call them? — episodes before. I worry for Mair. She thinks she can control him, but I'm not so sure. And they're alone together all the time in that weird house of hers, her spinning all day…'

2: Credo

Spinning! The threads of life. The weavings of myth glittering in warp and weft of contemporary narrative setting; the old stories that have their genesis in human response to the land.

155

Place here has an objective, a recognizable reality, as do the people who inhabit there. In 1973 I went to live in an isolated cottage, Brithdir Mawr, a mile or so from the head of Cwm Pennant, which becomes in the story Cwm Blaen-yr-Afon, encircled by the long ridges of Eifionydd, stretched out against the sun or under the moon. *'Bro ser hefin'* — 'Land of summer stars' — is how the sixth-century poet Taliesin described this region. They are so obviously old, these hills, worn down, picked bare, ancient, bald, entrenched in their own being, lived-in. At dusk orange skeins of neon braid their shadows; in daylight cloud swathes them reverently; perhaps nowhere is more beautiful? In one of Krishnamurti's dialogues there is a poignant exchange on beauty. A bewildered engineer confesses to the sage that though he is told a tree is beautiful, he cannot feel it so. In reply he's instructed in the watchful quietude from which appreciation stems, in which sensitivity intensifies, through which the voice of authentic experience speaks.

I'm reminded of a line by T.H.Parry-Williams: *'Mae lleisiau a drychiolaethau ar hyd y lle'* — 'There are voices and phantoms throughout the place.' Everywhere among these northern Welsh hills, even within the smallest compass, the range of reference is extraordinary. To many visitors, unacquainted with the culture, inattentive to the signs, it is often obscurely inaccessible. The writer, conversely, must be steeped in tint and dye of place. Take that valley into which Bethan and Bryn look down from their hill-top — Dyffryn Nantlle, the valley that runs up to Parry-Williams's birthplace. My memories centre around characters like Dafydd Nantlle, with his white hair and piercing blue eyes, cycling off before daybreak on an upright black bicycle with a long, single-barrelled shotgun slung over his back, and returning at noon with a couple of foxes and a rabbit or two dangling from the crossbar. Or Mrs Myfanwy Williams of Nantlle Terrace, garrulous and hospitable octogenarian in her back kitchen, who would tell you what she'd learnt as a young woman in the 1930s on WEA courses run by the poet Robert Williams Parry.

Dyffryn Nantlle is associated too with one of the key achievements of European literature, *Math fab Mathonwy*, the final story of the *Pedeir Keinc y Mabinogi*. It's a long, complex bundle of themes, embodying many folk-tale motifs, handled by its final anonymous redactor with remarkable skill and fluency and rooted in the features and place-names of Dyffryn Nantlle. Its Jungian shadow lies across my story.

A back road from Mrs. Myfanwy Williams' Nantlle Terrace leads through the old Dorothea quarry workings to Talysarn, where, from the pulpit of Capel Mawr, John Jones, Victorian Calvinistic Methodist minister, thundered out thrice every Sunday from the pulpit of Capel Mawr his self-denying ordinances. Close by, a blocky little memorial at the village crossroads reads 'Robert Williams Parry 1884-1956'. Here's the last couplet from one of the latter's sonnets, cast in the form of question and response between a visitor who's heard the *Mabinogion* story mentioned above and a resident:

> *Clywsant am ferch a wnaeth o flodau'r banadl*
> *Heb fawr gydwybod ganddi, dim ond anadl.*

(They've heard — of a woman he made from flowers of the broom,/Without much conscience in her, only breath.)

Here's the woman's joke shared between Bethan and Eleri. *Cydwybod* — 'conscience' — the target at which John Jones's strictures were unerringly aimed from Capel Mawr pulpit, in the hard light of which the

157

beautiful reduced at best to the merely moral, more often to the dubious and immoral. That opposition between poet's sympathies and pulpit strictures is made more plain as you follow Bryn and Bethan up the climb to the watershed ridge that bounds Dyffryn Nantlle to the south, beneath which is Cwm Pennant. Here's Williams-Parry again in his most famous sonnet, after chapel in fleeting encounter with a fox up here on this sublime ridge a hundred yards from the hill summit, seeing him as I have seen him so often, caught in poised surprise with one paw hesitantly held up, keen muzzled and the fires of his eyes upon me:

Llwybreiddiodd ei ryfeddod prin o'n blaen.
(the rare wonder of it appeared before us)

The sonnet itself is a watershed. It looks anew not on the return on investment in God, which message thundered out from the pulpit below, but on the work of God that is nature. *'Ei ryfeddod prin'* — the rare wonder of it!

Wonder is proper to a writer on place. Through the years I lived in Cwm Pennant that sense of wonder grew on me. Here was a landscape where every field-corner was thick with ghosts, where generations had played some cosmic chess-game, arranged and re-arranged stones into the temporary shapes of two or three hundred years, borrowed from here to build there, let frost and wind collapse and the grass wipe clean. It is a valley vibrant with the life of nature. Peregrines nest on Craig Cwm Trwsgl. How many times have I seen the tiercel attract the falcon from her nest, she flying under him and upside down to catch the pigeon he dropped to her, then breaking away to the inaccessible ledge as he sported round her. Foxes, too — supposed to be so alert, yet one passed me among the summit rocks of Moel Hebog one morning, coat glistening rich chestnut in the just-risen sun, my dog and I quite still and he not ten feet away so that his acrid stink had my bitch quivering in excitement.

Nor were hawk and fox the only hunters here. There were summer nights on the river when the foxglove bloomed and 'Owen John Cwrt y Cadno' and I patrolled our favourite water, where I held the lamp and carried the heavy battery as he poised, *trifar* in hand, fiercely intent, eyes flaring-cold as any soldier's hewing limbs at Pilleth or Mortimer's Cross five hundred years before; then the shaft's plunge into dark pool, thrash and gleam of the stricken fish. Once the bailiff came along, two women with us that night and no chance of escape. Two of us hid behind a bush, fish and lamp among the roots of a tree. Owen John and his friend were on the grass, she wriggling out of her knickers and pulling him down on top of her when the bailiff flashed his lamp: 'Oh, sorry mate, have one for me while you're at it!' And away he went.

These people — models for those of whom I have written — were as much a part of the spirit of the place as river or hills: old faces, lingering conversations, the companionable crises of the farmer's year — the frenetic sweat and itch of stacking hay in a barn, pandemonious sadism at the sheep-dipping, the shepherding — that time in the late snow, the sheep tired with long labour and no option but to bare your arm to the elbow, push the breech lamb up and round before pulling it out, the lamb and your arm both marbled bloody and yellow against the white ground; and a few days later, in a field which the warming sun had now patched with green, a hare reared up to box with this same lamb.

I remember the young man from the 'hippy' colony at Tanygraig who, desiring to live off the land's bounty, gathered the roots of a riverside plant and grated them into his salad. It was hemlock water dropwort. Within an hour he died in agony. His ashes were buried in the churchyard of Llanfihangel y Pennant, on the left as you enter the gate, under a painted slate. I remember talking with old Mr. Morus of Gilfach, asking him why sheeps' heads hung in the trees above the stream by his house: 'Duw, it's cure for the *pendro*. When the sheeps die, I cut off his head and hang it there. Blowfly lays eggs, maggots eat the brain, fall into the stream, and the sickness is washed from the land.'

Here is the land-memory; but you'll not find beliefs like that current if you go to Cwm Pennant these days. It has changed. A stiff knot of baling twine secures the rusting chapel-gate. Acre-millionaires and seekers of subsidies bought into the valley. My old friends no longer farm their land, now fenced around with wire. Grey wintering sheds of corrugated iron dominate. It is made to work to repay investment in it. Do I, rather than this exploitation, prefer the old unease at its beauty, which spoke at least of the mystery of the place, and of a certain reverence?

This is the land of summer stars, yes, but also of the stony pasture and the rough hills, the ravens' guttural cry and joyful play in the rage of the wind, the ermined stoat stuttering across the scree, the peregrine's stoop. In the after-light beyond sunset when the colours glow at their fiercest there's the emerald cushion of moss, on it a pearl-grey corona of feather and down, splash of bright blood at its centre still sticky to the touch and the falcon chattering against nightfall from her rock.

The four years I spent in Cwm Pennant were the most formative of my life. The surrounding circuit of hills, from Moel Hebog over Moel yr Ogof and Moel Lefn, then crossing Bwlch y Ddwy Elor — the pass of the two biers — to gain the 'Ridge of the Red Cairns' that stretches from Y Garn above Rhyd Ddu to Mynydd Craig Goch by Nebo, is Eryri's finest hill-walk. Throughout the years I lived here, I walked some part of this circuit, in the course of the shepherding by which in part I earned lodging and keep, almost every day. To have that closeness with a natural landscape is a life-changing experience, taking you into dimensions previously unsuspected, initiating you into the earth's mysteries, re-instating the old human senses that urban civilization has atrophied.

It was a time of gifts, and — in its way, though perhaps more in retrospect than when in process — of spiritual discipline. In all weathers, in all lights or no light, at all seasons, these hills became my intimates, disclosing, confiding. I slipped among them in the company of chough, raven and peregrine; of fox, polecat and hare.

I came to know: where, in the moonlight, the hares would race and box; crepuscular habits of the shy roe deer whose slots lead back into the forest below the ridge; by what paths badger and stoat would cross the twilight fields below the mountain wall; or on what rocks the rose-root and the burnet rose, within what streamside spray the hay-scented buckler fern, might grow. What the walking did, then and now, was to establish what I cannot but see as the most crucial, fulfilling and redemptive relationship of my life — the one on which all others depend and from which they have taken their contexts. Thoreau — incomparably the greatest of writers on nature and the wild — puts the view to which I hold most succinctly. Heed him well — here is the necessary creed for the writer-on-place:

> To ensure health, a man's relation to Nature must come very near to a personal one; he must be conscious of a friendliness in her; when human

friends fail or die, she must stand in the gap. I cannot conceive of any life which deserves the name, unless there is a certain tender relation to Nature.

[Journal, January 1858 in *The Portable Thoreau*, p. 590]

On a bright summer's afternoon of the present century I turned up into Cwm Llefrith from just above Cwrt Isaf — Cwrt y Cadno in my story. The little farm where my nearest neighbours and friends the Owen brothers — *'hogiau Cwrt Isaf/ the lads of Cwrt Isaf'* — had lived with their mother, who had no words of English, and which once would have been busy and thriving with animals and activity and children, was deserted, silent, tidy. But high among the rock bluffs of Cwm Llefrith and alongside the splashing stream bright heather and gorse were in bloom and the rarer plants too. I re-made their acquaintance as if seeking out old friends. At Bwlch Meillionen I left my sack behind a rock and raced up to the summit of Moel Hebog to see the peninsula curving out west into the lowering sun, Mynydd Enlli offshore at its end, Ireland's coast faintly beyond and Pembrokeshire's hills far away to the south. I remembered coming up here with my son Will in a baby-carrier on my back when he was two years old, waving his arms around and tugging at my hair. So long ago now. On the descent a bright, crescent moon glided out from behind Hebog, and I slipped back by riverside paths in the dew of evening to where I was staying in a caravan under Snowdon with a Daoist sense on me of the oneness of the Way, however wandering.

A few weeks later I was coming down from Caer Caradog in the Shropshire hill-country. The light of evening was filmy, moisture-laden. It was streaming through Lightspout Hollow and Ashes Hollow and

Devilsmouth Hollow on the prime bracken hill of the
Long Mynd opposite:

> Ah! well I know my tumultuous days now at their
> > prime
> Will be brief as the bracken too in their stay
> Yet in them as the flowers of the hills 'mid the bracken
> All that I treasure is needs hidden away.
> [Hugh MacDiarmid, 'Bracken Hills in Autumn' in (eds.)
> Grieve and Aitken (Penguin, 1985, II). *The Complete Poems
> of Hugh MacDiarmid*, p. 1152]

I was reciting MacDiarmid's verse as I reached the
lower woods; thinking of Will and his love of solitary
hill-wandering, his passion for the quiet times and the
infusing light. There was an ancient, decrepit hawthorn
across the slope to my left, leafless, stark. Suddenly the
flooding sun reached it. Its lichened angles glowed
emerald, the sparse haws on its branches brilliant as
garnets. 'Blood of the hosts' these stones are called in
Gaelic, their gift in folkloric tradition the mystical
communion, the moment of knowledge that the unity
of life can only be forged by love, to the birth of which
Thoreau's *tender relation to Nature* for me is surest
witness.

3: Veni Creator Spiritus

*No single venue but an infinity of gifts; and what is it of
ourselves — of our soul-expressions, our consciousness, our being
— that we will leave in these places?*

Hear what I'm trying to say here? To bring place to
life in your writing, it must be *your* life, your awareness.
To be a casual visitor, a day-tripper, a borrower from
books will lead you to be as shallow, as emptily
assimilative, as all those vacuously inauthentic and
bourgeois 'new nature writers' of the Cambridge

School — straining like constipated lexicographers, seeking to annexe others' experience, desiring only to impress — upon whom the metro-literati bestow their meaningless and ignorant praise. Place must have its due. You must let it answer the need in you, and not in token fashion. How telling that the voguish metro-term for what's beautiful is *stunning*. Don't be stunned — be conscious, alive, supremely aware. As Richard Jefferies, W.H. Hudson, Henry Williamson — the great tradition in English nature writing — were vitally aware at every nerve-ending, in every plucking synaptic discharge.

One Saturday afternoon early in July I thought to head down to what for me had long been one of the habitual places — one to which I'd often gravitated, where I'd slept out over the years on innumerable occasions. It's in Radnorshire, my favourite among the old Welsh counties, the quietest of them, sweetest of memories, secluded somehow, with soft green and rounded hills and wide horizons unlike those of any other part of the country. Here, in the crook of the Wye where it flows down from Builth then veers round easterly to pass Hay and head out of the high country for Hereford, is an insignificant group of hills looking across to the Black Mountains southerly and the Brecon Beacons to the west. These little hills go by the names of Rhulen, Llanbedr and the Begwns. Among them is a pool above the farm of Gogia created nearly fifty years ago to regularise its water supply.

It has yet to appear on any Ordnance Survey maps, but now looks entirely natural. It's surrounded by a copse of Scots Pine, the trees nearest to its margin dead, their roots drowned. I found the tortuous green track along which you arrive at the pool and lurched across its dips and gullies to park hidden from view among the drowned pines. The stump of a grey willow in the water itself was putting forth strong shoots, with leaves silver-felted on their undersides that gleamed in late sunlight. Bulrushes at the shallow end of the lake blended into a collage of green and copper and tawny and chocolate, round their bases the stems of reeds slipped on crystal capillary rings. It was absolutely still, not a breath of wind to stir the surface of the water. I put up a little green tent and sat quietly outside it for a time, watched moorhens, and a pair of tufted ducks glide and dive, lost to view at times in the low sun's dappling reflection. Swifts skimmed the water, leaving little spreading ripples as they drank in flight, then soaring and hawking in screeching pursuit of insects. As they tore past the willow-stump, a tiny goldcrest alighted there and wheezed its native protest. I gathered sticks, of which there were always plenty in this place, cut a square in the turf, made a hearth round it with stones, lit a fire and when the bed of charcoal was glowing set on it the wooden-handled frying-pan I'd used for these occasions since Will was tiny. The flames crackled and leapt and the resinous wood spat and sent the sparks whirling high. A night-jar was churring away, its pale form just visible, from a tree by the boundary wall of the farmland beyond the end of the pool. Flame of a candle placed against one of the drowned trunks rose unwavering, the bark-texture beautiful in its illumination, embers of the fire still glowed outside the tent as I subsided into sleep. In the bright morning I scraped the charcoal together, blew it into life and piled more twigs on until the flames leapt once more, fried eggs, cut and buttered bread, made coffee, spent the morning and most of the afternoon simply looking at the close textures of landscape. Then, in the still of evening, I walked up to Ireland.

It's east of the high point on Llanbedr Hill between Painscastle and Rhulen. This ruined house is a resonant

165

place for me. I first came here on a solitary walking tour of Wales when I was fourteen. Then it was sound-walled, roofed, windowed, abandoned. I pushed open the door, explored inside, fetched water from a cold and cress-lined spring, lit a fire of ash-twigs in the hearth, swept the wooden boards, spread my sleeping bag across them, sat on the doorstep to watch the shades thicken and hear the owls.

I sat there again next morning, cradling my tea as the sun rose through a gap in the hills above Colva. This was more than fifty years ago. All that's now left to maintain some pretence of uprightness are a few feet of cracked chimney breast, a mound of rubble, nettle-girt beneath the trees.

For half-a-century I'd wondered who had lived here? Until, reading a delightful book called *An Idler on the Shropshire Borders* that recounts the adventures and encounters of Ida Gandy who lived in Clunbury from 1930 to 1945, suddenly there was a glimpse of Ireland's former life. A keeper lived here, Mrs. Gandy tells us, 'a really kind and friendly man, interested in other birds beside his own game. He showed us where a ring-ouzel was nesting in the heather, and a pet raven whom he'd rescued when it had fallen from its nest.' She tells further of how the keeper's wife spoiled the bird disgracefully, feeding him biscuit meal from a spoon.

At Ireland once more, on a glowing evening with heather and gorse in bloom and the air fragrant with their honeyed and coconut scents, it seemed this couple's kindliness had long imbued the place, was what had drawn me back time and again over decades. As I left a curlew flew through the ash grove, heading for the mawn pool above where the shooters have their deadly lair, calling as it went, putting an ache of music to words from *The Secret of the Golden Flower* that were singing in my mind:

166

Whoever has done good in the main has spirit-energy that is pure and clear when death comes… The pure and light energy rises upwards and floats up to heaven, and becomes the fivefold present shadow-genius or shadow-spirit.

[*The Secret of the Golden Flower*, tr. Richard Wilhelm, foreword and commentary by C.G. Jung (Routledge 1931), p. 29]

Which is to define, in formulaic and doctrinaire fashion, what we may become and live, when we put aside interference from relativism, ego, borrowed and tawdry response, and attune our own consciousness to the startling, quick beauty of nature that surrounds us; when we have come, as Thoreau insists, into a tender and loving relationship with all natural life: which is the mystical union to which religions aspire; from which true writing comes. It is this simple.

You could wrap yourself
in a map like this one
Jane McKie

When I opened my eyes I saw nothing but the pool
of nocturnal sky, for I was lying on my back with
out-stretched arms, face to face with that hatchery of
stars. Only half awake, still unaware that those
depths were sky, having no roof between those
depths and me, no branches to screen them, no root
to cling to, I was seized with vertigo and felt myself
as if flung forth and plunging downward like a diver.

[Saint-Exupéry, 91]

It is a desert that gives the title to my first Cinnamon
collection, *Morocco Rococo*. The opening section of the
book, 'A Game of Four Winds and Sand', is all about a
particular landscape, the Moroccan Sahara. I trekked
through the Sahara in 2005 for Maggie's Glasgow; it
was an adventurous proposition for someone who
hadn't been outside Europe up to that point. Initially,
my impression of walking through the desert was of
scale and apparent uniformity, which, after looking
carefully, was not uniform at all but full of unique
contour, colour, and sliding footfalls of sand. The only
sign of private property was a pair of gateposts missing
their gate and wall, perhaps the residue of a grand
house that had succumbed to the red hinterland. In my
poem 'Fancy Gateposts' the posts stand on their own,
not exactly forlorn, but rather like two solitary 'out-of-
work viziers' who:

> don't connect
> to anything;

not a fence there
to declare even the most tenuous boundary.

A desert is another of the earth's ever-shifting seas. It is incredibly difficult to map the moving peaks and troughs of sand because the Saharan winds, what I think of as 'lonely dogs', keep things fresh: dislocated and alienated themselves, they blow atoms of whatever crosses the Sahara in 'a game of four winds and sand'. The four winds are the harmattan, a dry dusty wind from the Sahara blowing towards the West African coast; the haboob, a strong wind that occurs along the southern edge of the Sahara; the sirocco, a hot and dusty spring wind that begins in North Africa and can reach as far as Europe; and the khamsin, another spring wind blowing from the south. In an unfolding sandscape, the trajectory and speed of dust is as pressing as the need to cover the head, to hydrate the body. The wind as well as water (or its absence) has power over life, just as it does at sea.

I was dwarfed in that environment, made brittle by heat, leached of all sense of scale. The only maps to hand were landmarks residing in the heads of guides: maps, yes; but maps for experts only. For this reason, all the irrelevancy of life, its clutter and any self-importance, fell away. I was dependent on the goodwill of strangers, and humbled by the possibility of losing myself in that immense place. The night sky in the desert was equally overwhelming. Roasted and then frozen, I pulled my coat tighter and looked up at vivid, pulsing stars to experience the mirror of my daytime dislocation. What had once felt fixed — that homely, cosy sense of place — had become unmoored. It was vertiginous in the way Antoine de Saint-Exupéry describes. The sky was an inverted desert.

*

Another landscape that, like desert, resists physical colonisation but is a prime candidate for imaginative colonisation is Rannoch Moor in Scotland. In my next Cinnamon book, *Kitsune*, in the poem 'Rannoch' (first published in the Mariscat pamphlet, *Garden of Bedsteads*), Rannoch Moor is a 'wilderness peopled by ifrits':

> The first a hinny, horse-headed-mule-legged, running
> with a sideways gait
> against the wind. She brays. Stops.
> Brays. Stops.
> Her teeth are the yellow first light on a lochan.

The second is 'an orange-eyed rowan, small berries / the quickbane of an autumn coupling.' And the third is a fire, a 'thatch of russet grasses. / They gutter the whole year.' Djinn are creatures from Islamic and pre-Islamic Arabian mythology; they are hidden from sight and made of smokeless fire, and ifrits are a class of infernal djinn. Rannoch Moor with its sere grass, its pools and its bog cotton is another, almost alien, landscape that requires something — some intrusion, some otherness — to throw its grandeur into relief. Instead of wild dogs, I put a kind of demon to work to summon the power I experience on Rannoch Moor.

The idea of a being composed of smokeless fire seems fitting: on moorland the grasses do gutter, and the cold does burn. In literature, ifrits are also shape-changers. In *One Thousand and One Nights* there is a story in which one changes into the shape of an animal, into fruit, and into fire until it is reduced to cinders. This otherworldly, spiky and spitting malleability seems to me a good metaphor for Rannoch Moor through the seasons, all its shifts and patterns grounded in elemental power. It is through the process of transposition that I am able to express my feelings about the place. There is a relationship of strangeness, estrangement even, but also of equality and balance between the elements of the poem: the hinny and the lochan; the rowan and autumn; the wildfire and renewal.

The intractability of landscapes that, like Rannoch, are hard to inhabit, promise much to my imagination. Desert and moorland are emphatically what they are, they feel essential, and they have strongly identifiable and uncompromising personalities, and yet their territories and boundaries are difficult to fix. I am fascinated by 'what lies in between', all places that are equivocal and mixed, whether it is because they are inhospitable and difficult to map or simply because they resist classification.

I have always found borders to be charged with magic. In the poem 'Borderer', I identify border people as 'the best sin eaters', claiming that they are able to eat territory 'from both sides', to 'alter lines on maps'; passing over 'is coinage in life / as well as death, they say', meaning, of course, that sin eating is a commercial proposition but my intention is also to allude to a permeability/mutability of physical and spiritual, perhaps the most fundamental border. That particular dialectic has fascinated me since I was a child growing up beside an edge-land, the littoral margin between the South Downs and the English Channel, where, in my poem 'Crocodile Fashion', sisters are 'scalded by the smallest waves':

Unable to leave this marginal place,
they babble about their fear of the deep,
dancing the unstable plank between
dry land and sea, unaware of the tick-tock

almost snapping at their backs.

And it *is* impossible for me to leave 'this marginal place' behind. It was here, in this landscape — a beach of pebbles and grey sand near Worthing — that I first wrote at all, and, like every writer with their home, I still carry it with me. It is the place I can summon immediately, without much effort, if I close my eyes. It is the place that retains its sensory qualities in my memory: taste, touch and smell at different times of year and in every kind of weather. It is familiar: I am bored by it. It is familiar: I am comforted by it. It is familiar and, now I have left, it is full of surprises.

On the coast, serendipity is part of life: things wash up, and wash away. One is a legendary bell, the Sussex Bosham Bell, associated with the small coastal village of Bosham where, it is speculated, Canute commanded the waves to retreat. The tenor bell, stolen from Bosham church, is said to have slipped from an invading Danish longboat into Chichester harbour, ringing out as the other bells were rung to sound an alarm. While its first tolling was supposed to have destroyed the retreating ship, it still rings to accompany the surviving bells in the poem 'Bosham Bell':

> [...] My call is plaintive, you
> answer in kind. The tedium of repetition
> has rusted my tongue
>
> and now each peal is softer than the last.
> Diminished conversation might pain you.
> I look forward to letting it go.

This is a poem about relationships in the quotidian of course, but it is also about our diminishing conversation with the past, and the action of time on our stories: if they are not written and rewritten, told and retold, they will fall out of discourse and fade away. I remember the 'Local History' section of my local library being crammed with curling brown pamphlets, or books with seventies photos and badly designed covers that were only ever consulted by octogenarians. And me.

In wanting to celebrate the old stories adhering to places I know well, I am guided by my reading. Someone very much rooted in place was George Mackay Brown, the Orcadian writer whose poetry and prose can be read as hymns to those islands and their peoples. In his novel, *Beside the Ocean of Time*, the protagonist is Thorfinn Ragnarson, and his vicarious journeys mimic the process of reading empathetically, of letting people and places filter into the imagination until we feel them, or, more than that, they become internalised.

In the final chapter of the novel, after the Second World War, Thorfinn returns to an island deserted and divested of its identity (it was used as an airstrip during the war, the islanders relocated) to search for his authentic first imagining, his lost 'eye of childhood'. Ironically, the lazy, dreaming boy was the poet and the full-grown man a writer of 'historical romances' who had somehow mislaid his original poetic voice. At the end of the novel, Thorfinn attempts to recapture that original voice, to 'dredge something rich and strange out of the mythical past of the islands — the selkies who shed their coats on the moon-blanched sands and danced; the trows who live under the green knolls and love above all the music of men, so that they cajole young fiddlers to their courts inside the hill and keep them there for fifty winters' (p.209).

Like the traditional story, Mackay Brown's writing is a legacy and a living gift, and I love its rootedness in a kind of narrated history that has more or less fidelity to its sources depending on the purposes or whims of its author, but which never fails to celebrate the narrative quality of thought. Writers like Alan Garner or Tove

173

Jansson, who also draw on powerful senses of place and history to furnish their imaginative fiction, have long been favourites of mine too.

My childhood home is a curious mix of local legend and suburbia. A good story has perennial appeal, but what about suburbia? I think suburbia, another littoral place, begs to be slightly skewed in imagination. In my imagination a garden pond wishes for 'black kohl to line its ordinary eye' ('Fancy Dress'), and misfits can't sit still 'on beige floral settees, knees together', wilting in 'storage heat' ('Fourteen'). There is a clamouring for glamour to suburban living that is perfectly in keeping with an adolescent preoccupation with identities, with trying out different versions of self in fantastic ways. It is almost as if suburbia *is* a teenager, wanting desperately to be a grown-up city. Yes, it can be stultifying, but where oddity exists, it feels magnified a hundred-fold by the unremarkable context.

Worthing is a seaside 'retirement' town with Regency pretensions, with down-at-heel arcades, emptied lido and Italian sea-front cafés. In a town like this, a life can be lived out in comfort or squalor and never create so much of a ripple on any landscape, cultural or otherwise. Triumphs and vexations are weathered discretely in a context of relative peace and prosperity. And at the edge of it all is the sea, a magnificent salve, so attractive to an ageing population that they flock to it, just to feel the sun and salt on skin and to sigh at the sight of that lovely long horizon. And why not? It is enough.

I miss it now with a low dull ache, miss the daily walk by the sea and the chance for thoughts, and time, to stop racing. It has got to a point where I don't even remember why I wanted to leave as soon as I left school. It was the done thing to go out into the world and find your fortune, Dick Whittingtonesque, I suppose. The working of imagination on the memory of a place can render it increasingly palatable through a weeding out of the bad and a preservation of the good that erases complexity in such a way that the objects of memory begin to take on idealised qualities. There is an aspect of this to the way I remember Sussex-by-the-sea. In *Kitsune*, the 'I' of the poem in 'Empire of Sundaes', set in an Italian seafront café, is scathing about nostalgia:

Sweet, corrosively sweet,
this urge to live in the past,

to guzzle a fizz of days
spent in a shallow pool

that lingers on the palate
more potent than the days themselves.

But this is disingenuous. Nostalgia is a potent force that can be mined productively by a writer. At times psychologically hampering, nostalgia is nevertheless authentic for the one who experiences it, and I would suggest it has the power to evoke mood and atmosphere in a way that can be especially fruitful for more associative writing. Of the Sussex poems in *Kitsune*, one in particular is very rooted in my early memories of a cherished place: a chalk garden I have visited and revisited many times, so much so that every detail has been polished under scrutiny. But in my poem, 'The Infernal Garden', the garden is less shiny, more ambiguous. I take something bright and deliberately obscure it in order to impart an atmosphere of menace: the taken for granted is sinister. It can be extremely dislocating when a comfortable environment

175

is divested of its perceived safety, particularly for a child. I am lost in my 'blue jumper / knitted with wormy wool – / too warm for Sussex in the '70s' and everything is changed:

> bushes have sprung up
> along the path, its brickwork
> spiralling towards gaping carp,
> those ageless, pig-lipped brutes.

In this poem 'childhood is migraine' and the place I love has transformed into a forest. The more I revisit a place in my mind's eye — rehearsing all its properties — the more I take liberties with it as a writer. I feel it somehow belongs to me by virtue of acquaintance, and fidelity to an accurate, hand-on-my-heart-this-is-how-it-was representation becomes increasingly irrelevant. Is this growing confidence as a writer? Is it impatience? I'm not sure.

I have taken liberties with another cherished place in this new poem.

The Pools

> There are so many pools. From above, they're pores
> on weathered upland skin. Ruffled by wind, they're
> the ferrous hue of a fox's haunches — indecently rich
>
> under a grey-rinsed sky. I wonder why we've come,
> we're shivering like the rain-filled pits. Low clouds
> turn themselves to snakes, seeking tussocks tongue-
>
> first to disperse in. It's so unlike the stuffy chapel where
> we kissed. You lead, I follow, the bones of my face
> aflame with cold. I hate this place for its greater beauty.

176

Could you drown here? *You could. A sheep or two might've.*
But I listen to you call it God's land until, like a cultist,
I want to bide in iron and mist by the beds of red water.

The poem is set in a fictionalised version of the Teifi Pools in Ceredigion, Wales. In reality, there are only a few lakes rather than many pools, and they are not water-filled excavations. I never for an instant hated it. The Teifi Rivers Trust has this to say about that landscape:

> The lakes were famed even in medieval times for the quality of trout and eel fishing to be had here, and deep enough that at least one was believed to be unfathomable. They are still fished and (since their damming in the 1950s) now provide a drinking water supply for the surrounding area and the coastal belt of Ceredigion to the West.

> The landscape here is stark, wild, and extraordinarily beautiful.

Living not far away for a year in the '90s, I visited the Pools often. I was very happy; the landscape *was* a paradise to me, a place I could imagine settling in. Every time I went, I experienced the colours, all the russets and greys, palpably, feeling the gradations in tone — in reality a complex thing — as enormously simple, a palette so familiar it felt as if I could have grown up there. Something about the landscape claimed me, maybe because it is yet another sea of sorts. That's why I am surprised by the dark turn this poem has taken. It has gone through quite a number of revisions in which I have used the malleability of words to build a composite from different details, different observations made on different days. The rendering of real to fictional — even of something, someone or somewhere highly specific — must surely involve this kind of minute adjustment in order to convey an emotional truth. 'The Pools' started out as a highly Gothic Bluebeard poem and I needed to temper that to get the psychological and the physical landscape to meet in what I feel to be the right kind of balance.

In many ways, 'The Pools' exemplifies two aspects of my approach to writing about place. The first is an intensely visual way of looking at the world. I am drawn to art and to imagery in the writing of others, especially painterly imagery. The second is the role of the unconscious: I most enjoy poems where the representations they throw up are not the ones I expect. When I write — or read — it is essential I don't quite know where I am going to end up; I like it to feel exploratory, and I enjoy odd perspective, openness and ambiguity. There needs to be an invitation to inhabit a landscape and make it my own and I need to make several journeys: I think of writing as a map to be interpreted and explored, rather than a set of directions like a recipe, or sat nav. Directions render the whole process more formulaic and kill my interest.

In the 'Pools' the raised uplands with their shallow hillocks and deep pools are a cup for the sky. They reflect its colours as they might reflect a state of mind. A wild rather than an urban landscape most often prompts my associative thinking. I am drawn to poems and stories about cities too, and often wish I could write them with more conviction. Some great literature celebrates modernity and the city; I'm no eco-snob, although a reverence towards nature permeates my poems because of where I grew up and my early reading. At secondary school, for example, Wordsworth left an impression, specifically *The Prelude*, which was a first introduction to the notion of the sublime:

When, from behind that craggy steep till then
The horizon's bound, a huge peak, black and huge,
As if with voluntary power instinct,
Upreared its head. I struck and struck again,
And growing still in stature the grim shape
Towered up between me and the stars, and still,
For so it seemed, with purpose of its own
And measured motion like a living thing,
Strode after me. […]

The memory of the peak perceived in that way on that occasion provokes in Wordsworth a 'dim and undetermined sense / Of unknown modes of being'. Wild and ungovernable, this apprehension of mountains is a far cry from rolling South Downs and a relatively tame sea, but my desire to show the psychological through the visceral, the abstract through the concrete — that is a challenge I have always embraced and, more often than not, my attempt is charged with a sense of immanence. Although they are rarely explicitly religious, I often write poems that could be described as worshipful, if only in the broadest sense of the word.

It was the tangible embodied sensation of crouching to look though a low-set window in the wall of a particular church, St Mary the Virgin at Burpham, that set me thinking again about place and time. Already moved by the place, the act of crouching and peering brought home the disjunction between the medieval paying of obeisance and the way in which we can so easily overlook remnants of that time. So while the 'contagion' of the lepers has 'lifted' the 'low glass':

remains, but their breath,
their rash, their lack,

179

has passed into the lace
of shadows in the yard.

Where God looked
but did not touch,

the lip of sandstone
is purled with fissures.

In 'Leper Window, St Mary the Virgin', the natural erosion of the sandstone is recast as present day physical evidence of the position of lepers in medieval England, of both their need for charity and their perceived pollution. What I hope to achieve is a blending of physical and spiritual in a way that is not dissonant but which gently picks up on the irony of tension between the two. It is not an irreligious poem – if anything I am becoming more devout in my determination to map wonders.

You could wrap yourself in a map like this one. This is the opening line of the poem 'Montgomeryshire, Scale Six Inches to One Mile' in *Morocco Rococo*. In this poem, the place and the person fuse through the mediation of a map: the map clothes the naked body like a skin. As large as a blanket or a cloak, it is comforting as well as sensual, a tactile object that forms a delicate but robust layer between flesh and grass. This poem is a fusion of macrocosm and microcosm, not entirely serious, in which 'your tummy' could rest on Tregynon and 'your pubic bone' on Aberhafesp. But at the end I circle round to the place in which the poem was written: 'when you shift your body's contour / around the creases of the map, Bron-Hafod Dingle / above Gregynog could become the perfect *omphalos*.' It is the centre, the navel; it is the point from which creation might emanate.

I became a little obsessed with maps of wonders, especially mappa mundi, when I co-tutored an Open Studies course on paradise gardens at the University of Warwick. We focussed on Persian, Chinese and Christian gardens, finding through our reading that the Persian and Christian gardens use descriptions of paradise to underpin their mandala design. 'Montgomeryshire, Scale Six Inches to One Mile' is followed by, and closely linked to, the poem '*Mappa Mundi*', based on the thirteenth century Hereford Mappa Mundi in which the Garden of Eden is located in a circle at the edge of the world, with Jerusalem at the centre as the map's omphalos. But it is Eden where my focus lies: walled and battlemented, it is surrounded by a ring of fire. It is simultaneously of the earth and inaccessible to mortals. Adam and Eve, 'crudely drawn', are just out of Eden, and I imagine them thirsty: 'Parched from exile, we will drink / the India of our Maker's ink'. Both poems contain self-conscious references to making that are reflections on how place is constructed. In a sense, we hold every place, whether directly or vicariously experienced, whether real or fictional, as a schema or map in our minds.

In *Paradise Lost*, Milton famously writes of man's 'First Disobedience, and the Fruit / Of that Forbidden Tree, whose mortal taste / Brought Death into the World'. To lose Paradise is to confront mortality. The loss of the first garden elicits feelings of nostalgia — nostalgia for a place one can only imagine. For centuries, men tried to locate the actual earthly site of Eden. Jean Delumeau quotes from an extract of Christopher Columbus's report of his third voyage (1498) in which he reached South America and was hopeful he had found Eden:

All this provides great evidence of the earthly Paradise, because the situation agrees with the beliefs of those holy and wise theologians and all the signs concord strongly with this idea. For I have never read or heard of such a quantity of fresh water flowing so close to the salt and flowing into it, and the very temperate climate provides a further confirmation. If this river [the Orinoco] does not flow out of the earthly Paradise, the marvel is still greater. For I do not believe there is so great and deep a river anywhere in the world. (p.55)

Residual nostalgia for the idea of Eden is a construct against which we can map our personal utopias and dystopias. Mary Warnock points to the way in which the nostalgia associated with the loss of an earthly Paradise could be said to correspond to the way we feel about lost time in our own lives, returning us to Wordsworth and the memorialisation of place: 'Turn wheresoe'er I may, / By night or day, / The things which I have seen I now can see no more'. Warnock feels these lines from 'Intimations of Immortality' have their counterpoint in memory:

But simply because the separation of past from present remains, there is in memory, necessarily a sense of loss: we look back to a country to which we cannot return. (p.141)

Rather than being hobbling and indulgent, nostalgia for what has passed, what is lost, can be productive. Although there is a sense of loss, there is also resilience — an act of resistance even — in remembering. Wordsworth used his memory and imagination to craft poems that transcended their context to address past and present with conviction. For me, so much of writing poetry is about reaching for something that feels just beyond arm's length, just out of the frame. The completion of a poem is not about something attained; it is constantly leaning towards and beyond. A place one has lived in or visited becomes intangible at the moment of departure; it is immediately a lost garden of sorts. Changed subtly or noticeably when visited again in the flesh or in the mind, a place can be thought of as an instant in time as much as a geographical location, and for this reason it cannot be rendered precisely. But it is in the attempt to bridge the gap between here and there, then and now, that the impulse to write lies.

Where I've always been
Gail Ashton

We moved house twice on the overspill, some of the first Brummies offered incentives to come off the city council list and fly to semi-rural outlands. On both occasions we found ourselves in villages holding their breath.

Redbrook Lane was nothing of the sort. It was a long strip of unheated local authority houses leaning against miners' cottages on the opposite side. One end clung to the skirts of a forest, a receding Cannock Chase. The other spat out onto a so-called main road and fields petering out across the well-worn track to the power station whose huge-bellied tower snorted soot and phlegm into a Staffordshire sky. I kept my back to that industrial open mouth, gazed instead at blue veins and tattoos writhing on the muscular marble of folded arms, men off the early shift, half-cut and leaning on front garden gates to soak up the last of an afternoon sun. I listened for the rattle of milk lorries trundling through the small hours on their way to the dairy near the single factory where dad worked, buried my head under the covers at the lonely refrain of trains rumbling and shrieking all night long.

Most of all I hankered after the Chase. You stepped onto it almost by accident. First scrubby twigs and branches, earth pock-marked with slack and scree. Then grass springing underfoot, tussocky, sweet-smelling rough stuff. This place was pitted with curranty rabbit droppings and other sticky substances. It had curves and hillocks and holes which whispered whiskery stories if you put an ear to them. In winter it was bog and peat and even on a summer's day its startle into saplings, trees, copse, woods, had its own cool tickle. I learned how to name it: oak, ash, conifer; birch, bracken, heather. There were rabbits, stoats, and weasels, strange flutterbyes, the bright glories of fox, secret dappled deer waymarking dreams, bramblings, bluebells, cuckoo spit, all the things I had read about in books and which now lived in my own eyes.

On the Chase night breathed with sharp yellow eyes and the wind spoke in tongues of pine needle, oak apple, berry. We didn't actually go there that much. It was *strictly prohibited* without adult company. I saw those words on a sign about spitting on the number nine going down the Ridgeway to Grandad's. We were allowed to the corner lamp-post, across the road to the Grattons, and up to George and Rita's house. We played out until someone finally noticed we weren't there. All the time the Chase called to me and I could not reply. Sometimes dad and George took us with them so we could roar and race about. It took me a long time to realise these were reconnoitre sessions, preparation for rabbiting which was why George's dogs came too. I sobbed and refused to eat another mouthful once dad told us the stew was rabbit, and his face and eyes went black again and he bellowed and tears and dinner were flung over the table, up the wall.

Most people think the west Midlands landscape is nothing much to write home about. It's still marred by its former manufacturing heyday and urban decay. Its towns are riven by iron, smelt, coal, chimneys, pistons, rush jobs. Its place names have the hard ring of furnace and forge: Brummagem, the Black Country, Darlaston, Ocker Bonk, Ironbridge, Tipton, Smethwick. This was the heart of an industrial revolution that Thatcher's Britain ripped right out. In the 1980s I drove through ghost towns gutted by the recession. Factories were scalped or demolished. Miners' collection boxes pleaded on every corner. A daily commute through Cannock and Littleton took me past a shrinking mine. The enormous colliery wheel vanished literally overnight. I had to pull the car over I cried so much.

Birmingham folk are of the Second City. But you'd never know it. While Manchester hollered when the IRA blew up the Arndale, Birmingham quietly cleared up after its pub bombings. Where we live is unprepossessing, or so we believe, *flatt-ish*, *all right-ish*, sometimes just plain old *rubbish*. We support the Villa or the Blues and if it's the latter then know regular despair: that Latchford was *bleedin' useless*, Kenny Burns alternately *diabolical* or a *godsend*, and that things had never been the same since we let Trevor Francis go. Few of us rate the magnificent redeveloped city centre with its gorgeous red-brick iterated in steel and glass, boulevards, the new Library square with its museums and theatres, Canal Street basin, the old telephone exchange. It took a lectureship at Manchester University and a move north before I finally got its unique appeal. Midlanders are a dry, self-deprecating people, consistently underwhelmed. *Aaarh, s'all right I s'pose* is high praise indeed.

No-one admires the Birmingham voice. Go on. Say it out loud. *Birmingham.* All flat vowels, slightly nasal twang, shrugged-off consonants. You don't hear it much in the media or carried across the head of a crowd in some place other than home. Even Black Country wallahs with their broader, altogether shoutier accent, despise us. Once, on my way back from teacher-training college in Walsall, the driver made an unscheduled stop on Ablewell Street. He threw a passenger off the bus with a *fuck off back to where yow cum from, yow bastard 021-er.** I travelled barely a few miles from home for my first teaching post. It might as well have been Timbuktoo. I was fazed by all the *yow wor, yow cor, yow am.* A shaven-headed lad kept asking me

186

to spell a word for him. Soon the whole class was miming it: *shert*. It took forever to dawn: *oh shurrt*, I said.

Brummie isn't a dialect or even an accent; it's an intonation. Like its lands its sentences fall away. Sound is close-mouthed, tight-lipped, faintly depressed. I worked hard to lose it and now hanker after its cadences. Some words still give me away: *butter, bath, cushin, tuthpaste, biskitt, I'm foine*, our dog's name, Lyra, sometimes misheard as *Lara*, just as asked to repeat my name in class I was once *Dale Ashdon,* not the familiar *Gay-ul* of home.

The west Midlands conurbation is knotted up in motorways and traffic and a proposed high speed rail link that will take a handful of us into London, ravage the last of the countryside. No southerner will use it to come to us. We can already access most places with ease. Most Midlanders don't bother. It's greener here than you might imagine. Like everything else, even the backstreets, sneaky cut-throughs and gulleys of its urban face, this part of us is below radar.

Every year since the Millenium I swear I'm going back. *Home.* This is the reality: I have no idea where it is. I laud Birmingham yet haven't lived on its inner ring since I was four or walked its crossways since I don't know when. The suburban outer circles our family once inhabited are as unappealing now as they were when I scurried away from them. Towns and cities make me feel biblical, *strange unto myself.* I have spent a lifetime trying to avoid confinement, longing for isolation, a place from which to watch incoming weather and light. It would take a king's ransom to tempt me back of my own free will. This is the thing about nostalgia: it knows you don't really mean it.

I am striding through town: Bullring to New Street, swing up to C&A, left into Colmore Row, past Lewis's, down to the old M&S, the tiny Seventh Day Adventist hall huddled on the corner of a street railed by bus stops — which one is mine? Dusk unpicks the cross-stitch of day. Flock after flock of pigeons swoops in to start up a noisome quarrel in the eaves of tall buildings. Starlings follow, a seething cloud swirling across a skyline. I could be in any city in the world.

I am huddled in the stables of Cedar Court, the big house our mom cleans in, playing hide and seek with my sister. Sunlight shafts the open slit of a gable-end high up and exposed to air. Wood pigeons coo-coooo nearby, soft as toffee, a fluttery silhouette of sound.

I am in a lift, tiny, pressed against knees, shopping bags, wet wool, cigarette-infused synthetics. I am hot in my winter coat, would like to tear it off, dart away, swallow, the name on my tongue, *a swallow*, the shape of it in my mouth. When we lurch to a halt I am afraid of suffocating, of being left behind. I cannot move. I sob into a buttoned-up collar of fake fur. Not a soul hears me.

I am on a boat carrying across to the Arran Isles off the west coast of Ireland. This is the last time I see my mother. She is standing in the prow, head half-covered by a hood, face turned to the salt-spray of a choppy sea, looking for all the world like the film star she always wanted to be, all around her burly men in cable-knit sweaters, oilskins, women with headscarves, baskets and boxes bucking with the motion of waves, provisions ramped down in pickled strata, cheeses, fruit, malt loaf perhaps, fresh vegetables, condiments, washing powder, hanks of bread. This is my mother and I cannot take my eyes off her. At the time I am looking at her, she will have been dead for almost thirty years.

I am in all these places and none of them. In time and out of it. I measure time and memory through birds: sparrows and robins dead of the cold, a kingfisher, the nuthatch nesting in our oak. These are the gaps into which I write myself. If this were an academic essay and me still in that world I would say I am liminal. Or else it's dis-placement, the hyphen a reminder of a slow unhinging borne of not fitting, of being out of place. Is this how we all start? Is this what compels us to write? To lose and find ourselves again in a place at once familiar, at once so eerie, jarring, foreign in every sense? And if you placed yourself there on purpose is this is how you might do it? Think of a place you know well. List what's in it. Use your senses to sharpen observations. Make your details concrete. Stay there a while. Now write that list again to tell yourself about the following: things that fall from the sky, that lie on the ground, are broken. What are the songs and stories you hear, the colours of their language? Tell a secret about that place.

This is my secret, the place from which I both write and cannot write. It begins with a breakdown but of course this is but a landing stage on a far longer journey. We don't talk about breakdowns much these days. I've had a few of them and I'd like to say that the label is important. A breakdown describes a world coming apart at the seams. Things fall through. Some of those things are lost. Others inhabit a different space-time continuum where they take on wondrous shapes and startling colours. They speak in strange tongues, have a scent of all their own. They are rarely entirely human, a bird perhaps, a trick of the light. Sometimes they beckon in others, something you haven't seen for a while. Strangers even. These things may or may not be returned to you. If they are, they often don't resemble themselves. If they do, you may be diminished in some way. The medical profession has a name for this country: bipolar affective disorder, type II. I know it by the song it sings: *home*.

Home taught me how to pay attention. Our chaotic household with its conflicts and high drama was no place just *to be*. The knack was to watch faces, gather the impress of a scene at a glance. Shouting back was an option in my teenage years. I spent so long observing others I forgot to look at myself. Even so, this quality of attentiveness is useful as a writer. I write about place obliquely: at a slant, through the prism of a slant. I write about home which rarely is, but more about what inhabits these homescapes, its people, its birds, animal life, the shapes of its landscapes, the tongues those landscapes carve out. This morning I see the same vixen I tracked all last year, her hole an old badger sett beneath the lee of a bridge. She's hugging the hawthorn hedge, intent on prey, just as last week she swayed along the dip of a stream, amber against a daylit snow. I recall the swing of her in summer coming down the fields, hot rabbit heavy in her jaws, breakfast for her babies, and I am glad I know her, that I know this place.

I write into the spaces I've left behind, that long-gone, illusory *home* shape-shifting through memory, imagination. It is pernicious and paradoxical and ambivalent. I write forward into a present-tense, as estranged from this mutation of a *home* as I'm rooted there. And on into all those prospective places, those passing-throughs, real or in my head, alternately receding and alive with possibility. These are places of lesser and greater safety, few of them anchored. In each of them people I have known, loved, rise up through a watershed of loss. They inhabit small worlds, shored there, yet not. They are refracted and unreliable. What does place mean to me as a writer? All of this dissonance, and more.

My first poetry collection for Cinnamon Press was *Ghost Songs*, its cover reminiscent of the view from one of my favourite canal bridges. It's a book rooted in memory, the vagaries of language, in myth. But it's also very much of its time and place. These poems came when I was just beginning — to quote one of its titles — to listen to its 'Sound Tracks', its waterways, bridges, banks and narrowboats, *Jimmy Mac* drifting down the slip of a canal. I watched herons, a kingfisher. I sat on benches and waited for the light to bleach out. I recorded these observations and detailed them in my work as though to capture them could lend a heft they didn't have in real life; for I was having a major episode at that time, walking the land the only way to make sense of a fragmentation that came in vivid bursts, colours of all hues, and a rawness, as if a skin had been removed and its inner scaffolding exposed to an abrasive air. For the first — and last — time in my life poems came almost complete, at a single sitting. In my head I was in the Wilbrahim Road chippy near the university. Or at Christie's Hospital, in Lyme Park, up on Pym Chair with the wind whistling through me in the Goyt Valley. I was 'Mrs' Noah in her husband's shed, their bedroom. On a rare childhood vacation in Wales, or locked out of a house while my mother sat drinking coffee and smoking round a neighbour's.

For a long time I thought *The Other Side of Glass* was a completely different collection. Now I sense that it is rooted in a similar earth. It veers between stasis, that shifting sense of home, and its call to a wild, to possibility. I was travelling for part of the time I wrote it, up and down the motorway on family duties, north, south, and sick of the voyage. At others I was just visiting, as we did when we were kids, and there is an attempt to hold things in place in its titles: 'On being alone in a school late at night,' 'Dunstanburgh Castle

191

Ruins,' 'Haworth,' 'Letter from Abroad,' 'Ellesmere Port,' 'Clare Island.' I wanted to capture a restless energy too and so the poems are on the move. They shift from stillness to flight. One moment we are 'Emigrating to South Africa;' another we are 'Driving Away' or in a 'B-Road Movie.' Voices drift in across time: someone standing in a kitchen, a garden, a dusty hall. Someone else at a basement desk, watching horses through the window, penning a letter from an outdoor cabin. Two people meet in a house, in the library stacks. Others stand in the *sodium shower/ of the single street lamp on the corner* ('End Point'), motor down the M6, or settle for *a view, of sorts* ('Between the Lines'). These are glimpses of a personal atlas in which place is at once everything and seemingly nothing much at all, pointers towards 'How the land lies':

> Soon you'll drive back into dawn
> the old way, worn, familiar.
> There are no maps for what's to come.
>
> We walk on through dust and disappearing
> feet, time unsteady in the hollow
> of a palm. If I crossed a border
>
> to meet you, who would see us run or know
> what histories speak, how a land lies
> so small and incomplete.

Some lessons you learn early. As a child it seemed that where you were from mattered more than where you were going. You might be from Erdington or Witton, Perry Common, the Wyrely Birch. You might be of Summer Lane, College Road, the Dovedale. If you were a Robinson then you liked poloney and betting on the horses. You had a piano in the front room, just in case, and an internal check-list of commonness which included the Ashtons — rough, feckless, drunkards. The Robinsons avoided the Jewish cemetery hidden behind the Ridegway's high stone wall and iron-work gate; they feared they might find themselves in there. The Ashtons despised the Kellys at the end of the grove, even though some looked just like them and shared the same Irish traveller spirit. When I was twelve my parents bought their own house at the posh end of town. My mother found a telephone voice and tried to vote Conservative. My father still had swarf in his hair and shouted the odds at union meetings. He would down ten pints then roll home to terrorise us again. At grammar school he imagined he was the only one with his backside hanging out of his trousers. He liked to brag that I spoke French, then said educating girls was pointless, that we were snotty-nosed kids who knew nothing of the real world. When I mentioned Oxford he banged his fist on the table and declared it wasn't for the likes of us *with its bloody la-di-da ways*. He never thought of himself as a stereotype.

I am lying on a Freudian bed of my own making. I hope they have secured the doors.

In 1979 I return from Italy to learn how grief settles on a body like dust. Later I will come to know how you can inhabit a place yet not be part of it. My mother had died that same morning, a few days short of her forty-first birthday. My sister and I leave home, move house four times in under five years. It has precedent, a pattern: almost four and I'm taken from great-aunt May to what seems like the end of the universe. I don't know this woman who calls herself my mother. Nearly seven and fled again, this time to a house haunted by the attrition of my parent's marriage and a real-life ghost. Coming twelve, hauled off the council estate just

193

as my dad has a punch-up with my grandad and half of our close family peel away; we never see any of the Ashtons again.

I find all travel difficult, have only ever felt at home in two places, Italy and Northumberland. I have never lived in either. I have a secret pastime, a distraction technique of sorts: I like flicking through *RightMove*, am drawn, a magnet, to estate agents' windows. Wherever we go I say *I could live here*. The reality of moving traumatises me.

September 2000. I am working in Manchester, living in Cheshire on the fringes of the High Peak. Christmas 2001. Or is it the year after? I'm in a queue at a large out-of-town department store, less than ten miles from our house and caught in that blue-white light of technology and extra-terrestrial objects. Parked cars glitter, as ice as the east wind that bites day in, day out. There is a credit card in my hand. I would like to use it. The person standing next to me is a stranger. So is the one the other side and the one after that. I see flakes of snow in a gauze beyond the plate-glass window. In a moment I will cry. I leave my basket on the floor and drive away, animatronic. This is how I pass for human, so out of place in such a place.

It has taken fifteen years to rootle into this landscape we found by accident, on our way to somewhere else entirely. It was vaguely familiar, its canal, old mine workings, its barges. I am tuned to the nuances of its speech, talk to people whose names I know, and they know mine. I have named it in my turn: Anson, Rams Clough, Ryles Wood, Weasel Wood, the milk track, the Cage, Sheep's Hill, the sky field. I know its setts, dens, holes, its tracks, dry-stone walls, grit-stone trails. Here a buzzard roosts on a pole. Hawks drop. Owls call me to sleep and back again. Perhaps they will hail you and *etch your name/ in owl-talk* ('Owl-talk,' *The Other Side of Glass*). A moon might follow you along a frozen canal whose surface is scuffed by debris, branches scattered as bones are scattered to winds that whip off apricot-coloured moors, the blue foothills of the Peak District. Weather comes with a ripple of light, a prick on the skin. Snow and rain face down on the path, inexorable as air. Hares start from grass, a heart-burst of bronze. I know where pheasants brood, how herons are solitary stones, where a badger might rumble through a hedge, its claws tick-tacking up our lane. I have seen a fox cub up close, casual in a haze of sun; baby deer tucked in a hollowed-out tree or startled on the fence line; watched deer, sent to make my day, smoke through a wood or a field.

I could walk out of our house, up to Lyme, and all the way back home, through the Roaches into Staffordshire. Or up to Kettleshume, the Goyt Valley, to Flash, right into Derbyshire, across its peat, crags, sudden waterfalls, its snow-cupped skies. I like the possibility of it. I could keep on walking, as I imagine I will do in the grip of an illness that urges me outwards, beyond myself, a psychic rupture I attempt to express in a poem inspired by the strange ragged stonework of a place built as both defence and escape — the medieval 'Dunstanburgh Ruins' in *The Other Side of Glass*:

> ...I came to north and east
> unnoticed, to taste the salt
>
> and bright, to track a gleam
> of washed-up snow,
>
> and feral me. The slip
> is stone on wreck.

195

I pray the dark will hold.
I've far to go across the waste

and no-one knows my name.

Here at home they must hide keys, boots, cash (it can't
be traced), listen to the restless pad of bare feet
through a night-time house, might find me hunkered in
a duvet, out of place, out of my mind. I tell myself I
would never really leave. Some nights it is touch and go.

The Cheshire climate is too wet for me, its skies ash,
silver, much too low. I don't always appreciate water. In
the 60s, the A34 murderer hid the little girls he killed
amongst the bracken at Seven Springs. We had
meandered along the stream there not so long before
they were discovered. In the winter of '63 our pipes
burst while we spent Christmas, as usual, at Grandad's.
Every day out seemed to involve a boat. We didn't have
many holidays. Instead we took numerous coach trips, a
charabanc, a bus to some place on the midlands dial for
the Ashtons hated being kept in, longed to be out and
on the move. We liked an open vista such as Malvern,
Lickey Hills, the Long Mynd. On the rare occasions
Grandad worked he sat in a deckchair taking money for
the tennis courts in the park. Like many landlocked
midlanders we had little interest in the coast, venturing
only to Blackpool, Rhyl, Weston-super-Mare, places
where the sea is so far out you might as well stay at
home. Best of all the Ashtons liked rivers, lakes; even a
pond would do. My dad's youngest brothers worked the
boats on Witton Lakes. Often they all went fishing,
from parks, to canals, to the famous rivers — the
Severn, Trent, the Avon, the Wye. Dad won
competitions and had an enormous fetid kreel rammed
with equipment. I could identify fish: perch, roach,
chubb, sometimes bream. Once I saw a tiny rainbow

trout drowning in a dried-up tributary. Another time I watched the Severn Bore rampage up and into Stourport. That was where Grandad and Uncle Dennis had their caravans and where we spent weekends raring round the weir, tramping sopping fields over to Arley, Bewdley, and back. We drank Vimto in beer gardens, our sneakers wet with dew, and dodged rats in the tunnel near the campsite after a knees-up or a ceilidh.

A visit to Stratford ignored Shakespeare, saw us on a river boat with a stripy awning and the wind in our hair. It was the same at Symonds Yat, Ross-on-Wye, Evesham, always a rickety pleasure-cruiser, a heaving steamer. Even a rowing boat was enough. Water. The Hereford plain submerged. Gloucester and Shewsbury part-vanished in brown floodwaters from the rivers I knew so well. Water. Devon Crescent, our second overspill house, with its beckoning fields, out-of-bounds canal and its pools, those disused sand and brick quarries. The Atlas was our favourite, steep-banked and slippery. It had newts, no bottom to it. It had pike, one so ancient it was the length of a boat, or so our dad said, would take off your hand or swallow a pup in a single bite. Once we waded through reeds and shallows in our wellies and hundreds of tiny frogs, some scarce bigger than a thumb nail, swarmed over our feet, and me and my sister squealed for the fright of it.

Water. The north-west. Its unblinking green canal. Its bogs, mud, its clags of earth. Endless rain, either mizzle or torrent, the constancy of it trickling off the moors, gathering, slipping underground to spout back up where you least expect it. I describe my years here as a time when the world seems less solid. I slip and fall, break bones, tear ligaments. I don't feel safe, in any sense. Locals say our house is built on an old pond. Sometimes I imagine the secretive underfoot course of it. Real or not, it has a certain truth.

197

Sometimes too I picture myself walking down Hawthorn Road and turning off the long straight of the Ridgeway into the side-streets and cul-de-sacs of my grandad's house. Number 3 Ripley Grove is still there, though my grandparents are long gone and we stopped visiting forty-five years ago after my granddad threw us out of the family home. My Uncle Dennis lives there now, or so I'm told. In this fantasy I unlatch the gate and stroll down the path to the front door. The expansive trunk of the felled elm tree sits outside the window. I knock and wait. I say, do you remember me? I know you, know the wardrobe in the front room where Grandad locked me in as we played hide and seek, just because he could. I know where the dog's kennel is in the yard and the lobby under the stairs with its old shopping bag full of your American comics. Know the pull-down in the kitchen too tacky to touch, the sugar and milk out on the table day in day out. Where the tiny Christmas tree wavered on top of old newspaper and other junk hoarded on the sideboard. How someone would draw the fire with sheets of paper to warm a bony backside in front of it after the match. All these things and none of them. None of them important and all of them threading our stories, our lives, our every conscious and unconscious utterance. This is why we write, to fix someone or something in place even as we know its impossibility. This is why my next work is — at long last — memoir, a reshaping of the stories of the past in order to re-imagine something of the places of the present. And so here I am, at the end, where I've always been — in the language of loss which shapes us all:

*

No-one ever let the dog in. She was marooned in the yard whatever the weather, sometimes hunkered far back in her kennel, at others padding the perimeter fence, a dozen loping strides on the far side, desultory circles near the kitchen wall, a half-curious pawing at the coal bunker, a single whoomph as she slid to the floor and leaned against the gate. Sometimes she moaned softly to herself. I thought it the saddest thing ever.

Mostly I sat with her. In bad weather or desperate for a quiet space, I ducked into her little house and curled up against her warm flank. She liked every book I liked. I read them aloud to her. Other times I perched on the closed lid of the outside lavvy and wished everyone dead. Judy's snout pushed open a door and her huge feet landed in my lap. She rested her bony head on my shoulder and we both cried.

She was a failed guard dog. Grandad kept her to watch over the yard with its useless mangle, rusting coal bucket and derelict pigeon shed. *Never trust the bloody Irish*, he said.

Mrs Kelly didn't like the dog. No-one did, except me. A visit to the toilet was a military operation for all the relatives, neighbours, and assorted drinking cronies gathered in the house. *Put that dog up Sid. I need to go.* Judy leaped at the door, bared her teeth in a friendly smile. She liked rapid movements. Once she nipped my cousin on the bum as he dashed for the sitting room. I thought it a job well done.

My nan clutches the broom, jabs at air. *Goo on wi' yer*, she shouts. Judy lays her head on the back step and yawns. Nan pushes ineffectually with the yard brush. *Bloody thing*, she says.

I say, *She just wants to come inside.* And inside my head: *if I was her I wouldn't bother.*

* *021-er* is a name given to Brummies. It refers to the old national telephone code for the city which was 021. People of the Black Country (wherever that is) are *yam-yams*, after their dialect version of the verb to be: *yo am...*

Afterword – Cinnamon is a Place
Jan Fortune

Place is at the heart not only of the books and genres that Cinnamon Press publishes, but of the press. Cinnamon is a place: being run from a family home — a quirky, oddly shaped granite house perched at the foot of the Moelwyns — gives Cinnamon a distinctive character as a small, independent publisher selecting books we feel passionate about; inventive fiction, poetry and non-fiction books that are not defined by genre, but by their ability to say something personal about their authors and to their readers — voices as distinctive as the place they are published — and so voice as place has become integral to our publishing project.

This is certainly apparent in the chapters in this book. John Barnie's rootedness in place, here, specifically Wales, is communicated in autobiography and poetry. Mark Charlton's love of particular places, Newcastle and Wales, informs his personal narrative and his relationship with his son. Jim Perrin confronts what it means to be part of a natural (Welsh) landscape. Ian Gregson takes us from working class Manchester to Vietnam. Hazel Manuel's personal quest goes from India to Paris and back. Sue Richardson tracks through Iceland and Pembrokeshire and considers what it means to put down roots. Jane McKie passes through borders — the Saharan desert, Rannoch Moor, the South Downs — and finds herself unexpectedly back in her childhood home in Worthing. Mavis Gulliver's connection to places is refracted through memory and honed in the Hebrides where she now lives. Gail Ashton, too, explores notions of home and personal crisis in Birmingham and the north-west; Jan Fortune highlights similar preoccupations in Wales.

Cinnamon's home is in a unique, slate-surrounded, beautiful, but feisty and raw landscape, and so we aim to include a significant list of Welsh writing in English amongst our titles, but this is a place that has a strong literary tradition, that has always drawn writers in, so we also aim to attract distinctive books from across the UK and the world. Our list includes books from Wales, Scotland and France and China and more... a cornucopia of voices bringing a wealth of places to bear on diverse texts. Cinnamon is a place that is open to the riches of many places, many voices. Cinnamon is a place where writers and readers from many places can wrestle with language or story or meaning or identity and this has been particularly exemplified in an on-going series of poetry anthologies that gather excellent examples of poetry in Italian regional minority languages and translate them into English. It seems particularly appropriate that a press nestled in a country with two languages gives a platform to minority language poets from elsewhere.

In the first volume of the series, featuring poetry from Sardinia, a small island that is home to ten minority languages, the poetry often centres on identity through geography, as Ignazio Delogu's poetry typifies:

Sa terra mia

  Sa terra mia
est una pedra
de sidis e de dolore
  Sa terra mia
est unu pane
caldu cantu unu coro
  Sa terra mia
est unu riu
de odiu e de rancore

Sa terra mia
est unu lentolu de gosu
pro su meu amore
    Sa terra mia
est una gemma iscurosa
pro su minadore
    Sa terra mia
est una luna
de ervas pro su pastore
    Sa terra mia
est una frina salma
pro su piscadore

My Land

My land
is a rock
of thirst and grief
    My land
is bread
as hot as a heart
    My land
is a river
of hate and feuds
    My land
is a lover's
sheet for pleasure
    My land
is a dark gem
for the miner
    My land
is a moon of grass
for the shepherd
    My land
is a briny sea-breeze
for the fisherman

The voices of these poets belong to a specific culture and location, yet they find expression in a press that gives voice from its own particular setting. Place and voice are as intimately linked as place and text, as Romangola poet and academic, Giuseppe Bellosi, writes in the third volume of the Minorities series:

IV

A i sral un pöst in do ch'j avânza e' segn
d'un at o d'un pinsir?
o a j armàstal sól
di sòni, dal parôl ch'al ve' int la ment,
ch'a' n'dis mai cvel ' t'vu dì?

IV

Is there a place that keeps track
of a gesture or a thought?
or do only dreams
remain, words that recur in our minds
never saying what we want to say?

Cinnamon is a space where voices can be heard and where text gives us clues to identity and meaning. To cite Donald Barthelme's 'aim of literature', Cinnamon is a place where there is the possibility of creating 'a strange object covered with fur which breaks your heart.' We hope the ten Cinnamon authors represented in the book you have just read give you a sense of how this might happen.

Writing: beginnings

Many of the chapters in this book offer ideas and suggestions for writing about place. Here writers share a few more.

Chris Kinsey

The habit of walking by rivers suits our greyhounds. They hunt sniffs and squirrels; I hunt for images and kingfisher sightings. They've taught me to see sharply in the moment and to stop striving for instant interpretation and quick definition. This helps my writing.

Frances Sackett

Paul Gauguin once said: 'I shut my eyes in order to see.' I think if you have a special place it's a trick you can always use to 'bring it back' — something you can tap into when you want some inspiration. Sometimes it will bring characters into focus as well as the spirit of the place. Also, if it is somewhere you have left and rarely gone back to, the focus seems even stronger.

Karen Maitland

I always create my novel settings from real places, so that I can visit them in different seasons and at night and in daylight. The place itself often inspires scenes and events in the novel — a drainage channel emerging from a mediaeval wall might give me the idea of someone being trapped behind those stones. An isolated church might inspire a lover's tryst that ends in murder.

When I explore a place I try to use all my senses. I consciously listen — could my character hear the river from here? Smell — what kind of vegetation grows wild here? Feel — at which point walking up this hill would my character first feel the sea-breeze on their face? I even try out actions in that place — how far across this graveyard could my character see by the light of a single candle? In that place I can become my characters.

Writing Tip: Decide from the beginning what the character feels about this place. Is this kitchen a poor but homely place to them, or a poor and miserable one? Select three items which would suggest either happy or miserable and have the character notice/remember those very early in the description. The smell of baking bread or a rag-rug will make readers feel the character is fond of the place. While if the character focusses instead on the broken, dirty window that will suggest he feels miserable there.

Jan Fortune

In his 1851 journal Thoreau wrote, 'The question is not what you look at, but what you see.' Go to a familiar place — a room, a favourite café, an outdoor place. Think about each sense and what you take from that place — sound, textures, sights, smells, tastes, but don't write anything down yet. Later, write a list of details about the place — make them concrete, specific. Write down everything you can recall — every taste, touch, smell, sound, sight; recall the time of day, the time of the year, how the light looked — everything.

Now write a piece that reveals a character through these details, without the character appearing. The writer always needs to know much more than the reader; so choose only the details in your place that are significant. Keep the language pared down, precise, visceral; aim for 'a strange object covered with fur which breaks your heart'.

Jane McKie

Get together with writing friends and make a composite map of a place cut from parts of other maps, sticking them onto a large sheet of paper to create a fictional place: either work together or take turns to write lines to describe each of the different locations, making a 'word map' to accompany the cartographical one.

Also with a group, pick a place randomly from an atlas, preferably somewhere you have never been. Pick a feature of 'place' and write a short piece on that element — perhaps its natural features (if it is a city, this could be a park, or if it seems unlikely to have any natural features, write about their absence). Pass this onto another in the group, who should write a new piece based on a different feature of the same place — maybe its *unnatural* features, such as a building or public space. This piece should also respond in a way that is in keeping with the sense of place initiated by the first piece. Continue passing on so the group constructs a fictional, composite place.

Get hold of unused postcards of a variety of places that you have never been — from unexciting to amazing — and write something short and pithy on the back, responding to how you imagine the places are on the basis of what you see in the pictures. Use your text as the basis for more developed pieces.

Pick a place that made an impression on you as a child and write extracts for use in a travel guide for it, using the categories *visit, eat,* and *sleep.* Make your recommendations simultaneously intensely personal and amenable to reading by an interested traveller.

Gail Ashton

Write 3 postcards from a place you've been to, in fewer than 100 words for each. Describe the following: something wonderful, something surprising, something terrible. Write in the second person — 'you', as though talking directly to someone.

Go to a place you know well and look at it again. Get an Ordnance Survey map (in effect, an aerial photograph) and compare it to what you see or have recalled of the place. List some of the place names which capture your attention. And/Or photograph it from every angle, close up and sweep. And/or focus on a natural object or two — a stream, a piece of quartz, a particular species of flower. Use your senses and these other props (map, photos, artefacts) to sharpen what you see, feel, hear, to explore further. Wait for the story.

Download and print a small map of a place you've never been to or know little about. Choose one or more features to focus on — places of interest, farms, woods, particular areas. Invent a story to go with that place. Begin with how you imagine it got its name.

Take a large sheet of paper. Write on it a short description of somewhere you know. Cut the sheet in half, vertically, wiggling scissors around so that you keep whole words. Swap sides, right to left, so the uncut sides are back to back. Shift one side up a line or two or three. Tape together. Use what you now have to springboard a new description.

Ian Gregson

Take a street map of the city where your novel is set. Make two copies of the map.

On one of the copies mark out the roads and squares where your scenes occur, then pin that copy to a wall.

Observe the spatial relationships that are created by this distribution of scenes across the city.

Imagine travelling between these locations, and the routes you would need to take.

On a second copy describe the features of these different locations: how do the buildings relate to each other? What angles of light cross these locations and how are they affected by the height of the buildings. From what angle will these locations be approached. How do they smell? Will different characters respond differently to them? Write notes about these questions on this copy, then pin this one next to the other.

Use the remaining unmarked copy to give yourself a sense of the 'bigger picture' composed by the marked copies, and place that next to the others.

Notes on Contributors

Gail Ashton has published fourteen books including two poetry collections with Cinnamon Press — *Ghost Songs* and *The Other Side of Glass* —, a biography of Geoffrey Chaucer and critical works on medieval literature. See www.gailashtonwriting.wordpress.com

John Barnie is from Abergavenny, Monmouthshire, but has lived for many years near Aberystwyth. His latest books are a collection of poems, *The Roaring Boys*, and *Footfalls in the Silence*, a memoir, both published by Cinnamon. *Wind Playing with a Man's Hat*, a new collection of poems, will be published by Cinnamon in 2016.

Mark Charlton writes about life and nature, describing his first book *Counting Steps* as, 'a response to the delight I've found in fatherhood and landscape; to the people I love and the places I find myself returning.' He lives variously in the West Country where he works and Wales, which has been home, on and off, for twenty-five years. A regular blogger, Mark writes at www.viewsfromthebikeshed@blogspot.com

Jan Fortune read theology at Cambridge, has a doctorate in feminist theology and has worked as a teacher, priest and charity director. She is the founding editor of Cinnamon Press, which she runs with writer, Adam Craig, and her previous publications include three novels and three poetry collections, most recently *Stale Bread & Miracles* and *Slate Voices* (with Mavis Gulliver). She lives in North Wales.

Ian Gregson's *Call Centre Love Song* was shortlisted for a Forward Prize. His 'Squawks and Speech' was recently on *The Guardian* blog 'Poem of the Week.' His novel *The Crocodile Princess* (Cinnamon Press) is out in 2015. Ian has published six critical monographs and is Emeritus Professor at Bangor University.See www.iangregson.co.uk

Mavis Gulliver has lived in The Hebrides since 1991 where she spends time walking, reading and writing. Her first poetry collection was *Slate Voices: Cwmorthin and Islands of Netherlorn* (Cinnamon Press, 2014, with Jan Fortune). Her second is *Waymarks* (Cinnamon Press, 2015). See her website www.mavisgulliver.co.uk which includes a Monthly Blog. Her children's fiction also has Facebook page s — 'Cry at Midnight', 'Clickfinger', The Snake Wand'.

Hazel Manuel is a UK born novelist whose writing follows a career in education, first as a teacher/lecturer and after as a business leader within the education sector. She now lives and writes in Paris where she hosts 'Paris Writers Working Lunches'. Hazel's first novel *Kanyakumari* was written over three trips to India and was the winner of the 2013 Cinnamon Press Novel award. Her second novel *The Geranium Woman* is published in 2016 by Cinnamon Press, and *Cliff*, a psychological thriller is her current work in progress. You can find out more about Hazel and her work at www.hazelmanuel.net

Jane McKie's first collection, *Morocco Rococo* (Cinnamon Press), was awarded the 2008 Sundial/Scottish Arts Council prize for best first book of 2007. Her other publications include *When the Sun Turns Green* (Polygon, 2009), and *Garden of Bedsteads* (Mariscat, 2011), which was a Poetry Book Society pamphlet choice. A new Cinnamon poetry collection, *Kitsune*, is published in 2015. She teaches Creative Writing at the University of Edinburgh.

Jim Perrin has written seventeen books and won many awards. *The Guardian's* country diarist for Wales, he is a Fellow of the Welsh Academy, an Honorary Fellow of Bangor University, and is currently working on a critical biography of the nature writer Henry Williamson. He lives mostly in the French Pyrenees with a tortoiseshell cat and a Parson Russell Terrier.

Susan Richardson is a poet, performer and educator whose third collection, *skindancing*, is published by Cinnamon Press (2015). She is currently poet-in-residence with both the Marine Conservation Society and the global animal welfare initiative, World Animal Day. Please visit www.susanrichardsonwriter.co.uk

Also contributing:

Jenny Cooke lives near Macclesfield, Cheshire. Amongst her books are *The Storm and Other Stories* and *The Cross Behind Bars* — Special Omnibus Edition (rep. 2003).

Miriam Darlington was born in Lewes, Sussex and lives in Devon. Her latest book is *Otter Country*. She writes for *The Times Nature Notebook* and tweets @MimDarling.

Sue Gregory was brought up in Derbyshire and now lives in nearby Cheshire. She has published four books for teenagers including *Martini on the Rocks* and *Kill-a-Louise Week*.

Emily Hinshelwood lives and works in south Wales. Her latest collection *On Becoming a Fish* (Seren) draws on her experiences of walking the Pembrokeshire coast, and is the basis of *Salt on our Boots*, a poetry, music and animation performance she has recently toured with harpist Delyth Jenkins.

Chris Kinsey has lived in Mid-Wales since 1979. She is the author of 3 poetry collections: *Kung Fu Lullabies*, *Cure for a Crooked Smile* and *Swarf*. Chris was BBC Wildlife Poet of the year in 2008. She writes a regular Nature Diary for Cambria.

Karen Maitland has published numerous medieval thrillers. Her latest books are *The Raven's Head*, *The Vanishing Witch*, and *Falcons of Fire and Ice*. She used to live in Lincoln but now resides in Devon. See www.karenmaitland.com or her regular blog spot on *The History Girls* website.

John McAuliffe's fourth book *The Way In* is published by Gallery Press (2015). Born in Co. Kerry, he teaches poetry at the University of Manchester's Centre for New Writing and contributes a monthly column to *The Irish Times*.

Louisa Adjoa Parker is of Ghanaian and British descent and has lived in south west England for most of her life. Her poetry collection *Salt-Sweat and Tears* was published by Cinnamon Press in 2007. She is currently completing a novel.

Frances Sackett was born in North Wales and now lives in north-west England. Her poetry collection *The Hand Glass* is published by Seren. In 2014 she was involved in Manchester's *Writing the Cathedral* project.

Joy Winkler, former Cheshire Poet Laureate, is a poet and writer working freelance as a performer and facilitator of creative writing workshops. Her latest collection is *Stolen Rowan Berries*. See www.joywinkler.co.uk

References

Ashton, Gail, *Ghost Songs,* Cinnamon Press, 2007.

Ashton, Gail, *The Other Side of Glass,* Cinnamon Press, 2012.

Abram, David, *The Spell of the Sensuous*, Vintage, 1997.

Barnie, John, *The Confirmation*, Gomer, 1992.

Barnie, John, *The City*, Gomer, 1993.

Barnie, John, *The Forest Under the Sea*, Cinnamon Press, 2010.

Barnie, John, *A Year of Flowers,* Gomer, 2011.

Barnie, John, *The Roaring Boys*, Cinnamon Press, 2012

Barnie, John, *Footfalls in the Silence*, Cinnamon Press, 2014.

Barthelme, Donald, in Olsen, Lance, *Architectures of Possibility*, Guide Dog Books, 2012.

Bellosi, Giuseppe,*Minorities Not Minority, Poets from Romagna*, Cinnamon Press, 2013.

Brown, Mark, 'My father freed art from the frame. Artists like Hirst put it back in again, says Mary Moore.' *The Guardian*. 28 February 2015.

Charlton, Mark, *Counting Steps,* Cinnamon Press, 2012.

Delumeau, Jean, *History of Paradise*. New York: Continuum, 1995.

Fortune, Jan & Gulliver, Mavis, *Slate Voices: Cwmorthin and The Islands of Netherlorn*, Cinnamon Press, 2014.

Garner, Alan, 'Lens and land,' in *The Author*, Summer 2011, pp. 47-8.

Gregson, Ian, *Not Tonight Neil*, Cinnamon Press, 2012.

Gregson, Ian, *The Crocodile Princess*, Cinnamon Press, 2015.

Gulliver, Mavis, *Cry at Midnight*, Cinnamon Press, 2014.

Gulliver, Mavis, *Clickfinger*, Cinnamon Press, 2015.

Klein, Naomi, 'We changed before, so we can change again.' *The Guardian*. 24 April 2014.

MacDiarmid, Hugh, 'Bracken Hills in Autumn' in (eds.) Grieve and Aitken *The Complete Poems of Hugh MacDiarmid*, Penguin, 1985.

Macdonald, Helen, 'The six books that made me.' *The Guardian Review*. 31 January 2015.

Macfarlane, Robert, 'From aquabob to zawn.' *The Guardian Review*. 28 February 2015.

Mackay Brown, George. *Beside the Ocean of Time*. London: Murray, 1994.

Manuel, Hazel, *Kanyakumari*, Cinnamon Press, 2014.

Massey, Doreen, *Space, Place and Gender*, Polity Press, 1994.

McKie, Jane, *Morocco Rococo*, Cinnamon Press, 2007.

McKie, Jane, *Garden of Bedsteads*, Mariscat, 2011.

McKie, Jane, *Kitsune*, Cinnamon Press, 2015.

Milton, John. *Paradise Lost*, edited by Barbara K Lowalski. Oxford: Blackwell, 2007 edition.

Perrin, Jim, *A Snow Goose and other Utopian Fictions*, Cinnamon Press, 2013.

Richardson, Susan, *Creatures of the Intertidal Zone*, Cinnamon Press, 2007.

Richardson, Susan & Gregory, Pat, *Where the Air is Rarefied*, Cinnamon Press, 2011.

Richardson, Susan, skindancing, Cinnamon Press, 2015.

Ricoeur, Paul, Time and Narrative, Volume 1, University of Chicago Press, 1990.

Saint-Exupéry, Antoine de. *Wind, Sand and Stars*. London: William Heinemann Ltd, 1939.

Smillie, Susan, 'Waves of change.' *The Guardian*. 11 December 2014.

Thoreau, Henry David, *Walden*, Dover Publications, 1995.

Thoreau, Henry David, *A Portable Thoreau*, Penguin, 2012.

Walker, Alice, *Possessing the Secret of Joy*, Vintage, 1993.

Warnock, Mary. *Memory*. London: Faber and Faber, 1987.

Whitman, Walt, *The Collected Writings*, NYU Press, 2007.

Wilhelm, Richard, *The Secret of the Golden Flower*, tr., foreword and commentary by C.G. Jung, Routledge, 1931.

Wordsworth, William. *The Collected Poems of William Wordsworth*. Wordsworth Poetry Library, 1994.

www.ingramcontent.com/pod-product-compliance
Lightning Source LLC
Chambersburg PA
CBHW060922250626
47159CB00008B/3115